THE CHARACTER REVOLUTION

RESTORING AMERICA'S SOUL

by

Rolfe Carawan

With contributions by Jo Kadlecek

LIFEMATTERS
P R E S S

SEATTLE, WASHINGTON

THE CHARACTER REVOLUTION

ISBN 0-9651624-1-9

Library of Congress Cataloging-in-Publication # 97-093942

Dedication

To my children,
Rolfe Ledrew III and Rachel Nicole,
and to your generation.
May this book inspire my generation
to leave you an example of a life well lived.

Acknowledgements

Jo Kadlecek: For all your talent, research and the invaluable contributions you made in the writing and editing of this book—thanks a million.

Bill Gibson: What can I say? You are not only brilliant; you are a true friend. Thanks for your help.

Mark Walker: You gave of your time and creativity to help me in this project. Thanks for encouraging me to go beyond myself.

Haas & Jaycox: For the outstanding cover design and layout. You guys are the best!

Pat Miller: For your typesetting expertise and advice. You're a real pro.

Lea Joan: *My wife and best friend. Thanks for all your love and support. Your example continues to inspire me!*

CONTENTS

PART THREE: Living the Revolution

INTRODUCTION

As a nation we have lost our common vision. The signs of crisis are everywhere. People are jaded, cynical and skeptical about life and the future. There is a poverty of confidence in the hearts of people toward their leaders. One scandal after another demonstrates the need for true character in those in whom we put our trust. Some leaders seem more interested in perks and position than in doing what is right.

People of good will and conscience are leaving the fight because of the overwhelming inertia downward. Who can blame them? When a leader finds the courage to do what is in the best interest of the whole nation rather than his fickle constituency, he gets the boot.

The family, the very institution that is to provide protection and the transmission of necessary values to children, is in critical condition. The alienation and broken lives caused by family disintegration manifests itself in our children's lack of respect, both for themselves and authority. Crime is a growing concern. Violence is being committed by increasingly younger offenders.

This loss of respect and brokenness is all too evident in one of the most important institutions in America: education. Many educators are not able to teach as effectively as they would like because the classroom is either a battleground or a therapeutic group session. Too many of the young people I meet are functionally illiterate. This, when high paying jobs are increasingly difficult to find and change so quickly that many jobs are *obsolescent*.

This book, therefore, is offered as part of the solution to these problems. A solution that is based upon exemplary personal character.

In the following chapters, I question many of the modern schools of thought: humanism, materialism, hedonism, nihilism, etc. I also question cultural and moral relativism, selfish individuality and valueless education. Instead, I have searched our history, finding much hope in the philosophies and writings of those who founded our great country.

I come to you as a fellow sojourner: "one beggar telling another beggar where to find bread."

I give a great deal of attention to Benjamin Franklin's list of thirteen attributes for living a virtuous life. His wisdom and insights lay the foundation for a discussion that I firmly believe is both relevant and crucial to the future of our society.

An inherent danger in writing a book of this nature is the certainty that I will fall short of the ideals, values and principles that I set forth. I am painfully aware of my lapses of character. Therefore, I come to you as a fellow sojourner: "one beggar telling another beggar where to find bread." I come as a husband, father, educator, businessman and professional speaker who is deeply troubled by the declining morality I see while traveling throughout our country. This book, then, is my small contribution to finding a rational, sensible and practical way to challenge us all to live virtuously.

As I experience the consequences of my own lack of character and observe the sad effects of a society caught in a character crisis, I cling to the hope that *there is a better way.*

I contend that there are natural laws in relationships and human behavior that, when followed, produce positive results for the individual and community. These relational laws find expression through personal virtues and character traits, which are specifically identified in Franklin's list. The negative values and philosophies I see dominating our culture have stirred in me a strong desire to incite a revolution: a *Character Revolution,* with far-reaching impact on our country's future.

May this book be a stepping stone to such a revolution. I invite you to consider my "call to arms" and join the cause. I invite you to become a rebel — a rebel *with* a cause!

PROLOGUE

Once Upon a Dream

As he sat around the fire watching the sparks fly heavenward, like fireflies dancing in the night, he could not contain his fascination. For years he had heard of Alexander the Great and his quest for an elusive Fountain of Youth. Could he succeed where the great general had failed? The prospect was intoxicating.

The news that Columbus had discovered a new world only fueled a vision that had dominated his life. The vision provided both motivation and purpose for a young man who was convinced that the elixir from the Fountain of Youth would give him what he so desperately desired: happiness, fame and success. Success that was eternal. He would be immortal!

The vision of one day discovering this fountain and benefiting from its powers affected every decision he made. He lived the dream day and night. Anyone who would listen to him got an earful of the hope, joy and life that awaited the person or persons who would commit to pursuing the vision. Juan Ponce de Leon was not only committed to the pursuit; he was consumed by it. He could see it and feel it in all he did.

At an early age, Juan had bought into the myth that material wealth, power and prestige would give him what his thirsty soul longed for, significance: a significance that would validate his existence and his quest.

Initially, no one would listen. They laughed at his ranting as if he were a lunatic. He soon realized that he would have to earn their respect and the right to be heard. As a young foot soldier, Juan's opportunity came during Columbus's second voyage in 1493 to Hispaniola. For nine years, Juan faithfully performed his duties and grew in stature and reputation as a soldier.

In 1502, as a captain in Hispaniola, Juan's opportunity to distinguish himself finally arrived. While serving as a soldier under Nicholas de Ovando, Juan performed well: so well in fact that he was soon named governor of the province of Higuey. Juan had now gained the esteem and approval for which he had so desperately yearned! Yet, feelings of insignificance gnawed at him.

"The Fountain," shouted a voice inside his head. "Yes! The Fountain," he thought. "That is the answer to my emptiness. If I find the Fountain then I will be satisfied." Just how this fountain was going to fill the chasm within, he could not tell. It just *had* to. Everything else had proven to be inadequate.

Because of his position and power, Juan — now middle-aged — found a much more receptive audience when he spoke of the fountain that would make the old young again. At long last, Juan sailed from Puerto Rico in search of the fountain that would at last quench his parched soul. Others, as desperate as Juan to find fame and fortune, followed along eagerly.

Within a month, the search party struck the coast of Florida. Juan and his crew were enthralled with its beautiful white beaches and lush vegetation. Convinced that the Fountain would be found here, the Captain and his men enthusiastically began their search.

Repeatedly Juan would remind the men of the pleasures that lay ahead. Desire for fame and fortune has blinded many a good person; it proved to be no less true with this seasoned bunch. Their euphoria had blinded them to the signs of danger that would have been obvious to more rational men.

The swampy terrain was first viewed as a mere inconvenience.

Fighting off poisonous snakes and alligators was part of the hazard of seeking immortality. Yet, ignoring reality can last only so long. What started out as a dream, Juan's beloved vision, soon became a nightmare. The sweltering heat, stagnant water and swarming mosquitoes became unbearable. Juan could scarcely find fresh water, much less the elusive Fountain of Youth.

Then the unthinkable happened. Fear and self-doubt began to invade Juan's thoughts. Though his own inner voice could be silenced, it was not so with the others. Grumbling and mocking were heard from the rank and file. Men discussed openly the possibility that they had been deceived: that there was no Fountain. Driven by the vision, though, Juan could not — would not — listen. Self-deceived, he demanded that they continue. He was going to fulfill this vision even if it killed him: even if it killed others. And it did!

When confronted by hostile inhabitants, Juan fought and killed to protect his dream, his precious illusion. It was easier than confronting the truth. Why? Because the truth hurts. The pain of facing reality was too great for Juan to bear. So the truth had to die to keep a lie alive. Truth is too often sacrificed when it interferes with our pleasures, hopes and dreams; but truth, in reality, doesn't die. Though we may try to kill it or deny that it exists, truth lives on. Ignoring that fact can be fatal, as Juan and many of his men discovered. Mortally wounded in the attack, Juan's pursuit of a lie cost him his life as well as the lives of others.

Disillusioned and physically exhausted, those that survived soon stopped searching. Some sat down and wept. Others sat down and died. The vision *had* been a lie! All they had been told was wrong. All the stories were empty promises, pure fantasy. As the gut-wrenching reality began to sink in, some became angry — others became resigned. With a shattered faith and depleted hope, the emaciated empty shells that had once been men returned home, broken and beaten.[1]

The vision died!

THE CHARACTER REVOLUTION

PART ONE

Inciting a Revolution

CHAPTER ONE
Encroaching Darkness:
A Cause for Revolt

Ponce de Leon's vision, however inaccurate, was the product of his world view — his inner thoughts. *Worldview* refers to what a person has come to regard as true: true about life, the universe, religion, human nature, etc. It is the lens through which we look at the world. Ponce de Leon's perceptions and inner beliefs about life created a view that prompted him to carry out certain actions, even unto death.

In the same way, our unique thoughts and beliefs form the foundation for our personal vision and actions. If our perception or beliefs are inaccurate, unhealthy or untrue, then we may easily embrace a false vision — one with consequences for the individual as well as the community. Consider Ponce de Leon, and consider a young man named Rowan.

When the Spanish-American War broke out, the War Department needed to get a message immediately to the insurgent leader Garcia, who was waiting in an unknown region of the Cuban mountains. Rowan was ordered to deliver the message. For three weeks, through incredible hardship, personal danger and untold difficulty, Rowan persisted until, at last, *he delivered the message*. His feat and determination became legendary.

What kept Rowan going when all seemed lost? Why would he persist when others would have given up and returned to base? The answer can only be found in Rowan's inner thoughts, his worldview. His personal "vision" regarded performance of duty more important than personal safety. His honor demanded he continue even when no one else was watching. He valued commitment more than comfort. Rowan's vision of himself — the thoughts of his inner world — found expression through his heroic actions. Those actions inspired Elbert Hubbard to say:

> **We must *believe* the correct things, then act in a manner consistent with what we believe. It is true for individuals and it is true for nations.**

> My heart goes out to the man who does his work when the 'boss' is away, as well as when he is at home. And the man who, when given a letter for Garcia, quietly takes the [message], without asking any idiotic questions, and with no lurking intentions of chucking it into the nearest sewer, or of doing aught else but deliver it, never gets 'laid off,' nor has he to go on strike for higher wages. *Civilization is one long search for just such individuals. Anything such a man asks shall be granted; his kind is so rare that no employer can afford to let him go. He is wanted in every city, town and village — in every office, shop, store and factory. The world cries out for such; he is needed, and needed badly — the man who can carry a message to Garcia.*[1] [emphasis added]

How can a person become an individual like Rowan? The candidate must possess two things: 1) a worldview — or vision — that is true and accurate; 2) decisions and actions conforming to that worldview. He must believe the correct things, then act in a manner consistent with what he believes. It is true for an individual and it is true for a nation.

Five hundred years after Ponce de Leon's pursuit of an empty vision, we shake our heads and wonder how he could have been so foolish. Yet, in reality, de Leon was merely obeying his worldview, a view that included the deception called "the fountain of youth."

Many Americans are now beginning to re-examine their current worldview. Citizens are increasingly concerned that our great nation is coming apart at the seams. Civility, honesty, justice and order are fading away. Having searched for their own "fountain," in the form of personal peace (at all cost) and affluence (at the expense of others), many now sense that what they first believed, may not be true.

The vision that has come to dominate America in recent history, along with its corresponding actions, has procured some horrifying outcomes. Fathers are abdicating their responsibilities; marriages are falling apart at record proportions; mothers are doing the unimaginable: abandoning and even killing their own children; "babies" are having babies; children are killing each other; our educational institutions are languishing; and the future of the federal budget is, well, just plain depressing. It leaves many groping for answers.

Ours is a country whose identity is rapidly changing. Once known for its integrity and moral strength, we have spurned the very things that first gave us our reputation and influence. We are losing our sense of community, our respect for a job well done, and our commitment to the ways of honesty and virtue. We are looking more like Ponce de Leon than Rowan.

Perhaps British journalist Malcolm Muggeridge said it best when he astutely observed the plight of our western society:

> I disbelieve in progress, the pursuit of happiness, and all the concomitant notions and projects for creating a society in which human beings find ever greater contentment by being given in ever greater abundance the means to satisfy their material and bodily hopes and desires . . . The half century in which I have been consciously alive seems to me to have been quite exceptionally destructive, murderous, and brutal. More people have been killed and terrorized, more driven

from their homes and native places, more of the past's heritage has been destroyed, more lies propagated and base persuasion engaged in, with less compensatory achievement in art, literature, and imaginative understanding, than in any comparable period of history.[2]

Absolutely true. Numerous statistics prove it as well. Since 1960, our country has seen "a 500 percent increase in violent crime; more than a 400 percent increase in illegitimate births; a tripling of the percentage of children living in single-parent homes; a tripling in the teenage suicide rate; a doubling in the divorce rate; and a drop of almost 75 points in SAT scores."[3] What in the world is happening to us?!

The bad news: We have been pursuing a false vision — one that has precipitated a crisis of character.

The good news: Much of what is happening is self-inflicted and, therefore, can be self-corrected. It will not be easy; it will require most of us to make a radical commitment to a revolution: a *Character Revolution*.

Imagine what this country would look like if we held ourselves to a higher standard of conduct — virtuous living. We could restore what has been lost: our soul.

In our present crisis we, like Ponce de Leon, can continue pursuing a false vision that costs lives, or we can pursue a truer vision that produces a nation of individuals full of "Rowans"!

Turning Up the Heat

What is happening in the United States is similar to what happens when you perform an experiment with frogs and water. First, put a few frogs into boiling water. Right away, they will jump out, terrified at the temperature and in pain from the heat. Even frogs know better than to sit in the scalding liquid.

However, when you place frogs in water and *slowly* turn up the heat, what happens is quite a different thing. Being *cold* blooded, they will acclimate to the water and eventually boil to death because they do not perceive the danger around them — they cannot feel the gradual change.

That is precisely what has happened in America during the past thirty to fifty years. The water has been heating up and most of us have acclimated to it. We have become so numb to the decaying moral tide that we don't know enough to jump away from the danger. It has happened everywhere: Fraud, theft, greed, corruption and irresponsibility can be found in every institution in America. Untold pages of type fill our papers every day carrying the news of one outrageous act after another, while we ask ourselves, "What has gone wrong?"

From the halls of Congress to the pulpits of our churches, from our preschools to our universities, the temperature has been slowly rising.

Like Juan and his search party, we have not been paying much attention to what is going on around us. We haven't acknowledged the cause and effect relationship of our prevailing worldview. Moral degradation, philosophical relativism, and corporate cynicism have been "heating the water" of public sentiment for the past several decades. As the temperature rises, so do people's anger and frustration. Life has lost its purpose. Work appears senseless. Many live from regret to regret. Like a slow growing cancer, the disease of selfish indulgence is ravishing our national soul.

It is affecting us all. As former Secretary of Education William Bennett puts it: "This palpable cultural decline is the manifestation of a marked shift in the public's beliefs, attitudes and priorities."[4] As a result, many Americans are incapable of addressing the demands our current culture places upon us. We have not acquired the firm "beliefs, attitudes and priorities" necessary to cope.

Why have we failed to acquire them? Simple. We have become enamored with the temporal, material and superficial. We are increasingly concerned with only three people: me, myself and I. We are in pursuit of fortune or fame — our own "Fountain of Youth" — abandoning fundamental moral principles along the way. When we find a fountain, it is usually filled with bitter waters. Again.

To our own detriment, we rarely give much thought to the consequences of our selfish decisions. Immediate gratification seems to be the order of the day:

I want what I want when I want it.

If it feels good, do it.

Eat, drink and be merry, for tomorrow is not guaranteed.

You only go around once, so grab for all the gusto you can.

We want much, we have much, and we take much. All the while we give little thought to how our wanting, having and taking affects others or us.

American novelist John Updike said it like this: "The fact that, compared to the inhabitants of Africa and Russia, we still live well, cannot ease the pain of feeling we no longer live nobly."

> "The fact that, compared to the inhabitants of Africa and Russia, we still live well, cannot ease the pain of feeling we no longer live nobly."

Reversing the Damage

The water has been boiling, evaporating our sense of integrity and concern for our fellow citizens in the process. A lack of virtue in our personal lives has kept us from "doing good to man," what Benjamin Franklin called "the most acceptable service of God."[5] Without question, this has had far-reaching effects on our society.

"The West," observed author Aleksandr Solzhenitsyn in a recent speech, "has been undergoing an erosion and obscuring of high moral and ethical ideals. The spiritual axis of life has grown dim." Thus, our encroaching darkness. How then do we return to the light?

My answer is simple. Some might argue too simple. We must look to the *past* for solutions to our *future.*

In other words, the answer lies in our past, in lives gone before us. Our history is full of admirable individuals who were self-governed by proven principles and virtues — principles that produced tremendous results in their lives and in their communities. Their morals and values guided them to great heights of success. They blazed a trail for us to follow, if we are willing.

They became heroes: ordinary people who did extraordinary things because they relied on truths passed on to them by those who went before them. For the most part, they were moral people who lived normal lives as ministers, writers, statesmen, farmers, merchants, husbands, wives, mothers and fathers around the time our country was born. They knew that morals are those things that an individual comes to regard as the "truth" about what is right and what is wrong. These heroes in history (many of whom we will meet later in this book) learned, by example and by experience, that choices have consequences. They embraced the wisdom gained from others' successes *and* failures.

They teach us that the answer lies in what we regard to be true. As a general principle: What you believe to be true, you do! Therefore, it is extremely important to find the truth so that your decisions and actions will not produce the tragic consequences you want to avoid.

The Foundation

It has been said that we don't so much perceive the world as interpret it. Every choice we make is filtered through our belief system. That belief system affects our interpretation of the current perception, in turn affecting our emotions: and emotion is the catalyst for our actions.

Emotions and desires are overwhelming at times. Haven't we all faced the dilemma when what we know to be right conflicts with our desire to do otherwise? Can we believe something is morally wrong and still do it? Absolutely. Can we know what is right and still choose not to do it? Certainly.

A major problem for most of us is our lack of resolve to stand firm for what we know is right. Temptations fly at us constantly, screaming for us to compromise or do the expedient, even if we know it is forbidden. We deceive ourselves into believing that we are above the consequences and that we can do wrong without being discovered or punished. That is the wickedness of deception. An individual caught in deception's web does not even realize it, because he is deceived and blinded, even if only temporarily.

For the past fifty years, our society has tried to tell us that there is no good or bad, no right or wrong, no absolute standards on which to base our decisions. Morality is simply a matter of one's opinion.

Such relative "opinions" have created children who are morally handicapped and adults who have little moral courage. It's not that we don't have the inherent ability to make good, wise choices. It is, frankly, that the debilitating effects of this moral vacuum have rendered many incapable of recognizing the good, even when they want to.

> Under the guise of "freedom" and "rights," and at the expense of true liberty and happiness procured through wise decisions, we have become a generation of slaves.

Under the guise of "freedom" and "rights," and at the expense of true liberty and happiness procured through wise decisions, we have become a generation of slaves.

Ask the alcoholic if he is free from the tyranny of drink; the anorexic free to eat; the chain smoker free to stop; the drug or sex addict free to walk away from their vice. In all of our lives, there are habits and patterns of thinking that started out innocent enough. Yet, instead of being our slave, they become our masters.

Each of us can ask: How often am I ruled by my temper rather than my reason? Are my emotions ruling my behavior rather than sound judgment? Is my reason justifying insensitive and emotionally damaging behavior? Is my selfishness and self-centeredness taking advantage of others? Is greed overruling my honor? Are my ambitions overruling my commitments? All too often my pride has ruled, leading to the destruction of others and myself.

Have we forgotten that true freedom only comes when it is practiced with constraint: that individual rights are good only in the context of a community?

That is why it is imperative that we not only know the truth but also train our will to do what is right. Proven principles — rather than our fickle desires — should determine our actions. Principles, then, will dictate our choices and produce positive results.

Countering the Crisis

The tyranny of self, a disregard for the truth, and the loss of vision, community, dignity and character threaten our country's very existence. We must take up arms and fight.

Character development and moral fortitude will take us to a higher level, far above the rocky circumstances or tempting situations of daily living, so we can gain a better perspective. From that vantage-point, we can make better decisions, anchored in a set of virtues proven by those of character who have gone before us.

We are in a crisis of character and it will take nothing less than a revolution to get us out. LET IT BEGIN!

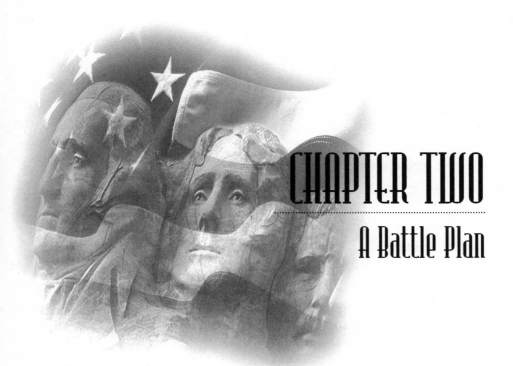

CHAPTER TWO
A Battle Plan

Revolution, by definition, means an assertively momentous change in any situation.[1] Obviously, the revolution I am proposing is not political in nature, but personal. It is an act of protest against the prevailing values that now dominate our culture. It is a rejection of those philosophies that promise freedom but have often enslaved us, making ours one of the most compulsive, addicted and neurotic countries on the face of the earth.

The first step toward turning our culture around, then, requires a thorough analysis of the opposition. In fact, to arrive at any solution, we must first define and understand the problem. Any military officer knows he must look at all potential conflicts and possible points of contention before constructing a proper battle plan. Likewise, it is important to look at the specific ways our country has experienced a crisis in character, so we can begin to counter it by a revolution of personal development.

Self, Self, Self

Few would argue that selfishness is a difficult rascal to whip. Without the proper development of character, our selfishness runs rampant. We lie to protect our reputation. We cover up the truth to avoid discovery of wrongdoing or mistakes. We deny to the end that we ate the cookie while the crumbs fall from our mouths. We steal to satisfy our self-gratification or because we feel as if we deserve something.

In a recent survey of 11,000 high school students, college students and adults, the Josephson Institute of Ethics found that cheating and lying are on the rise. Of the high school students surveyed, 65 percent said they had cheated on an exam in the past twelve months; 24 percent of the college students said they would lie to get or keep a job; and 47 percent of the adults said they would accept an auto body repairman's offer to include unrelated damages in an insurance claim."

Ethical problems arise when we operate on a low level of decision-making — feelings, desire and passions — instead of on the sure foundation of proven principles. The sensationalism we see daily in television and other media only exacerbates the problem. People shamelessly air their dirty laundry and outrageous behavior on national television — watch any talk show — until the perverse appears normal. Unfortunately, the toll in human suffering is nothing short of tragic.

Loss of Innocence

Consider the case of Yummy Sandifer, a ten-year-old boy living in a tough Chicago inner-city neighborhood. Yummy had been passed around from family members to foster homes to caseworkers. His need for belonging was so great that he joined a gang, trying to prove himself, and gain the acceptance he had yearned for all his young life.

His need for acceptance placed him in the crossfire of violent gang turf confrontations. With total disregard for human life, Yummy fired a pistol into a crowd of youths, mortally wounding an innocent young girl. Yummy went into hiding and for three days lived in absolute terror. Finally, the police found his little body under a bridge: Yummy had been shot and killed, execution-style, by two teenage members of his own gang. He had brought too much "heat" on the gang because of the killing.[2]

Long before Yummy lost his life, he lost his dignity and innocence. His beliefs, attitudes and priorities were sadly and immensely distorted by a world that taught him life had no value. Yummy's story, tragically, is not the exception these days; it's becoming the norm. It is a reality that surely calls for our collective indignation, inciting a revolution.

In 1994 alone, juveniles in the U.S. were murdered at a rate of seven a day, according to findings from the Justice Department reported in _US News and World Report_. This was an increase of three-fold since 1984! An estimated 2,600 youths were slain in 1994 across the country and 20 percent were killed by another child. Juvenile murders rose 47% between 1980 and 1994, while the number of total murders rose only slightly.[3]

It does not take a criminal expert to recognize that this tragedy has to do with a whole lot more than crime. These examples reflect a warped sense of values; a civilization that has lost its civility; a society that, with all of its technological progress, is losing its soul.

Ready to Revolt

Certainly, we are up against some pretty staggering statistics when it comes to confronting our culture's decline. The increasing numbers should be enough to thrust us into revolt. History reminds us that revolutions have always begun with a few individuals who had an idea, a thought, or a dream. A _vision_ of how things ought to be. In virtually every situation, the rebels believed that the overthrow of the existing system or authority would improve their position in life, as well as that of others.

Such an overthrow meant life would be better for all, more enjoyable for everyone, not just an elite few. Revolution would produce greater personal freedom and prosperity. I know of no revolts that occurred with the belief that things would actually get worse. Of course, history is also replete with accounts of revolutions where people did eventually find themselves in tougher situations than before. Their circumstances the result of a faulty vision or failure to appreciate human nature's capacity for corruption and selfishness.

Ideas Matter

The ideas I am presenting, as the foundation of this revolution, are not new — but old. They are principles, values and virtues that, if lived by, will enhance the individual and thereby change the country.

So what is our strategy for this revolution? We must focus our attention on developing our character for the good of others while fighting that old nemesis: selfishness. Within every individual lie the seeds for both good and evil, success and destruction, life and death. The seed that is nourished, watered, given light and cultivated will in time come to fruition. In reality, we choose which seeds will grow. If we cultivate "the better angels of our nature" sowing virtue rather than vice, our fruit will be sweet. Our choices determine the produce that will either sustain life or choke it out.

In essence, these seeds are the values, beliefs and principles that affect our decisions — and the inevitable consequences that follow. The dominance of the maturing seed will bring fruit that determines an individual's actions — actions produced by thoughts filtered through our beliefs. For it is through these actions, known to ourselves and possibly to others, that we define who we are — our character.

Character is defined by Webster's Dictionary as "a distinctive trait or behavior of a person who demonstrates their moral strength."[4] Essentially, your character demonstrates to the outside what is growing on the inside.

Let me say it another way: Who you are in the core of your being dictates who you are in your actions.

Character should not be confused with reputation. Reputation is what others perceive you to be. That perception may very well be an accurate estimation; it may also be an inaccurate or partial depiction. You see, private knowledge of our thoughts, beliefs and habits defines our character. Public knowledge of action defines our reputation.

I am firmly convinced that character is to be more prized than

reputation. A person's reputation can be marred
rumors or lies of others. Character maintains its in
of others. Simply put, our character is what we ar
watching. It is what we do even if no one else in
knows. Character dictates that we do what is right
right thing to do. Period.

Building the Weapon

However, character does not just happen: It is not an inherited trait; it
is not a gift or talent given or apportioned to the privileged few.

Character is color blind, gender blind and socio-
economically blind. It does not depend on
physical appearance, abilities or advantages.
Character shows no favoritism or partiality. In
fact, anyone can enjoy the advantages and privileges character affords. With character, lie the
intangible benefits of peace of mind, hope, purpose and meaning. Under character's care and
tutelage, anyone can increase his chances of
desirable consequences and decrease his
chances of undesirable consequences.

If all of these benefits and positive experiences rest with character, why then do we not
have more of it? Why is there so little empha-

> Simply put, our character is what we are when no one is watching. It is what we do even if no one else in the world ever knows.

sis for its need in our lives? Why do we see such a lack of character
in our culture? Frankly, I believe it is because few are willing to pay
the price for its service! Though character is more than willing to
work its wonders in our lives, it is very demanding. It confronts us
with the truth. It demands that we be disciplined and under control.
It asserts the right to restrain our behavior and passions.

If we are willing to submit to character's demands and require-
ments, we can experience a greater measure of happiness, fulfillment and success. As a society we will be safer, experiencing far less
crime and corruption. With character, we have the possibility of
becoming revolutionaries for positive change: famous, sought after,

esteemed. Without it, we become like the empty, gaunt faces of those who survived Ponce de Leon's expedition.

Developing personal character is absolutely essential for combating the cultural decline our country is presently experiencing. The results will be revolutionary!

CHAPTER THREE

Winning With "The Right Stuff"

> "The line separating good and evil passes not through
> states, nor between classes, nor between parties either —
> but right through the human heart."
>
> Aleksandr Solzhenitsyn[1]

Revolutions have come and gone. Each has left its own mark on history. Some have had an enduring affect while others received little attention. Some revolutions were violent while others were peaceful. Some procured personal freedoms; others brought bondage.

For instance, the Renaissance brought about enlightenment and new contributions in education, the arts and personal liberties. However, the Renaissance's inability to reconcile faith and reason has arguably weakened Western civilization to this day.

The French Revolution was supposed to be the answer to the common people's plight. However, if you did not agree with the prevailing version of political correctness, it could cost you your life. Tens of thousands lost their lives during the Reign of Terror.

Marx's Communist Manifesto was used by Stalin and others to enslave millions and justify the extermination of more than twenty million — all in the name of equality.

Hitler attempted to create a utopian society with his Aryan race, only to have it collapse around him. The death of six million Jews and hundreds of thousands of casualties from other countries are testimony to the devastating effects of a wrong belief system.

The American "sexual revolution" in the 1960s promised love and satisfaction. Though different in nature, this revolution has been as devastating as those just mentioned. Increased divorce rates, illegitimate births, single parent homes, abortions, sexually transmitted diseases and death prove that this revolution reflected serious naiveté. It has contributed significantly to the destruction of the family unit — the very fabric of society.

What lessons can we learn from the past? First, and most importantly, *beliefs and ideas have consequences.* Second, *revolutions that effect positive change are anchored in proper virtues, principles and truths.* Therefore, if we want to provoke a character revolution for the sake of our country's future, we must not focus our energy on possibilities, fads or trendy ideas. We must ground our efforts in principles that are tried and true. We must rediscover the truths that have sustained women and men throughout the ages and moved them to live well and for the good of others.

Laying the Groundwork

I find it fascinating that, compared to all of these revolutions, the American Revolution produced something unique. The blood spilt to purchase our liberty has left an enduring legacy. The absolute truths and principles upon which our Republic was built enabled a small band of citizens and their ancestors to become the most powerful and envied nation in the world. Their precepts were so powerful that, given time, they eventually eliminated the most evil of institutions, human slavery. The founders' ideals of justice, equality and liberty are still prodding us today!

The American Revolution was a reaction to injustices committed against the colonists by the English Parliament and the king. As Englishmen, the colonists looked to the king and Parliament to resolve their disputes over English rights and laws. Their appeal to

English common law was based on the "rights of Englishmen." These rights were spelled out in the Petition of Right of 1628 and the Bill of Rights of 1689.[2] When certain powerful members of Parliament began insisting that the colonists were not Englishmen and, therefore, were not to be provided with legal protection, the stage for dissolving political ties was set.

To make a legal case for such dissolution, the colonists had to appeal to a higher law. Prevented from any longer finding legal standing under the English constitution, the colonists had to appeal to a superior constitution; with no English judge to hear their case, they appealed to a higher judge. Their "rights of Englishmen" voided, they now turned to a greater system of rights. They turned to the "Laws of Nature and Nature's God."[3]

Sir William Blackstone's, _Commentaries on the Laws of England_ defined the "law of nature" this way:

> (W)hen the Supreme Being formed the universe, and created matter out of nothing, he impressed certain principles upon that matter . . . When he put that matter into motion, he established certain laws of motion . . . If we farther advance to vegetable and animal life, we shall find them still governed by laws . . . [The operations of inanimate and organic processes] are not left to chance, or the will of the creature itself, but are performed in a wondrous involuntary manner, and guided by unerring rules laid down by the Great Creator.
>
> . . . Man, considered as a creature, must necessarily be subject to the laws of his creator, for he is an entirely dependent being . . . And consequently as man depends absolutely upon his maker for every thing, it is necessary that he should in all points conform to his maker's will. This will of his maker is called the law of nature.[4]

This "law of nature" is the set of rules and rights guaranteed to every person, everywhere, by virtue of being a part of creation. It has been called the "Law of Right and Wrong." It is the universal constitution that sets forth the immutable laws of Right and Wrong.

It is the basis for the "unalienable rights" mentioned in the Declaration of Independence. These are rights that were endowed by the Creator upon man. Consequently, since the Creator gave these rights, they cannot legally be denied to any of His creatures. To do so is to deny a person their humanity.

Most people today think the term "laws of nature" pertains only to the physical laws of science: the laws governing physics, math, biology and chemistry. But the early thinkers had a much broader view that included moral laws. This Law of Right and Wrong (the "laws of nature and nature's God") could appropriately be called the Law of *Human* Nature.

> What makes man distinct from inanimate objects, animals and vegetables is this law of human nature: the law he can disobey if he chooses.

The concept is as simple as it is profound. Though man must obey the laws of science that govern everything physical (i.e., if a person jumps off a building, he will fall), man also has *another* set of laws to govern his actions — the Laws of Human Nature — which he can choose *not* to obey. What makes man distinct from inanimate objects, animals and vegetables is this law of human nature: the law he can disobey if he chooses.

Fortunately, when these natural laws are applied to human relationships and institutions, it allows for self-rule. Obviously, people who are ruled by a higher law do not need a monarch or state authority to rule over them. It means that the "law" was to be written on their hearts — and therefore obeyed.

The assurance that man can know and obey the laws that lead to success, liberty and happiness should be a source of great hope! It renews our optimism for a future that is rich with purpose and meaning. It offers a vision for living a beautiful life.

Free to Choose Beauty, Good and Truth

The ancient philosopher Aristotle spent a great amount of time contemplating what constituted a good life. So should we. In his writings, he discussed the three dimensions of man. Observing the three dimensions of physical objects — length, breadth, height — Aristotle deduced that people are three-dimensional: body, soul and spirit. He began to notice distinctions between man and his world.

- Man is a physical body but, obviously, more than just a physical body. We have unique characteristics that make us human beings.
- Physical objects take up space and can move in three directions: up or down, left or right, forward or backward.
- People do not only move in spatial directions; they move in intellectual, emotional and moral directions.[5]

As we ponder these distinctions we come to crucial questions in our discussion. *In which direction are we moving as individuals and as a nation? Which intellectual, emotional and moral standards guide our direction? If we continue in our present direction, where will it take us? Can we maintain this course and live well?*

Aristotle contemplated such questions. Perhaps that's why he suggested that man, being three-dimensional, lives well when directed by three natural standards: beauty, good and truth.

Beauty

Within every person there is an artist, a creator. Every man-made thing can be a work of art. Aristotle called all creations "poetry" because the word in Greek means "making."[6] The ideal is to create beauty in every human effort, moving beyond just the aesthetic works of music, paintings, drawing, sculpture, etc., to the production of practical necessities like furniture or clothes. When even the lowest esteemed jobs or tasks can be done in such a way that they bring true beauty, we are on our way to living well. In fact, every task, no matter how seemingly insignificant, can be done in such a way that it is beautiful and full of dignity!

Good

In addition to being creative, man is also inherently moral. That is, we have to make hard, ethical human choices, taking into consideration how those choices might affect individuals and society. Morality addresses what we should and should not do. It goes beyond just knowing right from wrong to actually doing what is right and avoiding what is wrong. It is comprised of the beliefs and practices that lead to happiness and few regrets. It is, as Benjamin Franklin called it, the art of virtuous living.

The moral person learns to consider his actions and what reactions they will create. Just as the artist wants to create beauty, the moralist wants to create goodness and harmony within himself and in his society. The only way to do this is to learn what comprises a good life and then act accordingly. That is why we must learn how to create beauty through what we make and goodness through how we act. To make these discoveries, we must know the truth about our human nature, our universe and ourselves. This brings us to our third dimension.

> Wisdom discovers the truth about how we best live with others. Wisdom acknowledges that there really is a thing called truth and that real truths are expressed in absolutes.

Truth

Man, the intellectual, is a learner — a seeker of truth — searching for and acquiring a wealth of knowledge. The search goes beyond the accumulation of mere facts to the proper application of those facts: this is called wisdom. Wisdom is the ability to take in knowledge with discernment, answering the question, "Is this consistent with creating beauty?" Wisdom discovers the truth about how we best live with others. Wisdom acknowledges that there really is a thing called truth and that real truths are expressed in absolutes.[7]

Fighting the Good Fight

Aristotle's idea of a beautiful, good and true life was the virtuous life — the life of right conduct. But how do we acquire such a life? Is it even possible for those of us living in such desperate times? Can consistent self-rule be at the heart of this virtuous life? I answer with a resounding, "Yes!"

As *artists,* not only can we paint a beautiful picture; we can do it with excellence. As *moralists,* we can be part of the solution rather than part of the problem. As *intellectuals,* we can pursue truth and the wisdom it offers, instead of stumbling along in ignorance, never discovering why life does not seem to work. We can choose a life of regrets — the result of faulty thinking or poor choices — or we can choose to live well through virtue and self-discipline. I believe the latter is the key to the character revolution our country needs. It is no easy task; we need all the help we can get.

Enter another great philosopher, artist and statesman: Benjamin Franklin. Franklin's dedication to personal character development allowed him to influence and shape the character of our country. As a result, he left a legacy of wisdom and insight: a challenge for those of us concerned about restoring the beauty, good and truth our country so desperately needs.

As you turn the page, you are taking a step in the right direction. I must warn you, though; the direction you will be taking is not easy. There is a cost. You will discover that the virtuous road, the higher road, is often difficult and narrow. If you take this road, you might be labeled a radical: a revolutionary. Yet, for those willing to risk, the rewards are great. Though you might not be popular, you *will* be in demand. You can help restore America's soul!

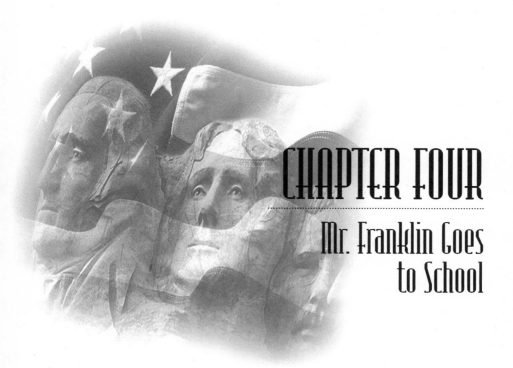

CHAPTER FOUR

Mr. Franklin Goes to School

If ever there was an extraordinary and peculiar figure in American history, Benjamin Franklin was it. Franklin's accomplishments during his long, productive life are what dreams are made of.

Franklin was born in 1706, the son of a Boston candle maker. By the time he was twelve, he became an apprentice for his older brother, James. James was a printer and newspaper publisher; young Ben learned a great deal from him, both about newspapers and business. Consequently, he wrote a series of essays for his brother's paper, calling them the "Dogood Papers."

At seventeen, an ambitious and restless Ben left his Puritan community for a younger, less rigid city known as Philadelphia. The City of Brotherly Love was good to him and he lived a rich, full life there as a statesman, author, inventor, scientist and printer until his death in 1790. Among his countless civic and scientific contributions, Franklin helped draft the Declaration of Independence, negotiated the treaty of peace with Great Britain in 1783, and wrote an autobiography that was the inspiration for this book. He wasn't born into affluence or prominence. He wasn't educated at the finest schools in the land. And he wasn't identified early on as gifted or set apart for some special calling. He never developed a "magic" formula for success. What made this eccentric and ingenuous man so successful? What was it about Franklin that caused some to consider him "the wisest American" ever?

Franklin found the one thing that mattered most to him. It is the one thing that still leads to true success. Franklin discovered that: *Developing personal character was essential for his own good and for the good of the society in which he lived.* He worked hard at living virtuously, setting high goals and standards of excellence so he could live a productive, fulfilled life. The moral of his story? Ben Franklin revealed (through personal character development) what an individual can achieve — regardless of family background, economic status or vocation.

> Developing personal character was essential for his own good and for the good of the society in which he lived.

The Art of Virtue

This one man's historical example has powerful practical implications for those desiring to see a character revolution turn our country around. Franklin was not perfect, but his commitment to improving his life and his country was irrefutable. Such dedication is worth emulating for those of us interested in obtaining success without regretting how it is gained.

That's why it is important to take a brief look into the mind of this wise American. Franklin was greatly influenced by the teachings of Aristotle and Jesus.[1] He was convinced that personal virtue was the source of true happiness. But it wasn't always easy for the prominent Philadelphia figure.

According to his autobiography, Franklin at one time believed there was no true distinction between vice and virtue.[2] In other words, he clung to a belief in moral relativism — that there was no absolute right or wrong. After a few years of floundering, though, he discarded the notion and concluded that there had to be intrinsic moral absolutes that governed the universe: "The Laws of Nature and Nature's God."

Franklin, holding firm to Socrates' maxim: "The life which is unexamined is not worth living,"[3] went in search of those virtues and truths that would be most beneficial to himself and others. Convinced that truth and absolutes existed, he searched for and found principles that offered individuals the best opportunity for success. Once identified, these principles were to be lived out in proper conduct.

This drive to live well was not motivated, as far as I can tell, by any formal doctrinal belief. Franklin was troubled by what he believed to be glaring inconsistencies with religious people professing one thing yet doing another. He struggled with the doctrine of divine revelation and the belief that God's forgiveness was a work of grace. To Franklin, favor had to be earned. His was a religion of works. Still, Franklin had great respect for his Puritan roots and for the Christian faith to which so many of his colleagues subscribed. Religion did a society good, he believed, and therefore had a useful purpose. Consequently, Franklin was deeply concerned about living a righteous, moral life, committed to virtues such as truth, sincerity and integrity.[4] This, he believed and later proved, would bring great happiness both to himself and to his community.

His was a very pragmatic approach to living a life of character. After much thought, he eventually developed a creed based on what he considered "the essentials of every religion." His creed considered "all the [religious denominations] we had in our country":

> That there is one God, who made all things.
> That He governs the world by His providence.
> That He ought to be worshipped by adoration, prayer and
> thanksgiving.
> But that the most acceptable service of God is doing good
> to man.
> That the soul is immortal.
> And that God will certainly reward virtue and punish vice,
> either here or hereafter. [5]

So, from this belief in accountability and reward, Franklin strove to obtain moral perfection. He set out to create a method for living a good and admirable life. He drew up a list of thirteen virtues that he deemed essential to the development of personal character for people of all religions and cultures. He then set about to integrate them into his daily life. Of such a plan, he wrote in his autobiography:

> It will be remarked that though my scheme was not wholly without religion there was in it no mark of any of the distinguishing tenets of any particular sect. I had purposely avoided them; for being fully persuaded of the utility and excellency of my method, and that it might be serviceable to people in all religions, and intending some time or other to publish it, I would not have any thing in it that should prejudice any one of any sect against it. I purposed writing a little comment on each virtue, in which I would have shown the advantages of possessing it and the mischief's attending its opposite vice; and I should have called my book "The Art of Virtue," because it would have shown the means and manner of obtaining virtue; which would have distinguished it from the mere exhortation to be good, that does not instruct and indicate the means . . . but it so happened that my intention of writing and publishing this comment was never fulfilled.[6]

Though "The Art of Virtue" was never published as a book, Franklin did develop his ideas and distribute them through other means. Some articles he penned for local newspapers addressed these virtues, as did a series of pocket size booklets called the "Dogood Essays." In his autobiography, Franklin suggests that he derived much of his work on virtuous living from a series of sermons by the Puritan preacher he long admired, Cotton Mather.[7]

Regardless of the source, Franklin's experiment, and goal to incorporate these thirteen virtues into his life, is commendable. The challenge for us is to do the same.

The Virtue Experiment

Franklin's desire was to live a faultless life; he was determined to overcome every wrong deed and inclination. So he set about to conduct an experiment on developing virtue. He reasoned that since he knew right and wrong, he could simply choose the right and avoid the wrong. He had found it helpful, as a young printer's apprentice, to draw upon the chart of virtues necessary for complete moral perfection — then to score himself daily on progress made or not made.

Mather himself could not have improved on the list of virtues Franklin drew up:

- Temperance
- Silence
- Order
- Resolution
- Frugality
- Industry
- Sincerity
- Justice
- Moderation
- Cleanliness
- Tranquillity
- Chastity
- Humility

For thirteen weeks, Franklin decided to track his accomplishments and faults according to the list of virtues he had devised. He thought, if he could keep a running tab of how he failed and succeeded, he could better understand the process of developing his character. He compared the process to "him who having a garden to weed, does not attempt to eradicate all the bad herbs at once, which would exceed his reach and his strength, but works on one of the beds at a time, and having accomplished the first proceeds to a second."[8]

At the end of each day, he examined the list to analyze how far he had come in shaping his character. "I determined to give a week's strict attention to each of the virtues successively. Thus in the first week my great guard was to avoid even the least offense against temperance, leaving the other virtues to their ordinary chance only marking every evening the faults of the day." You can track your own accomplishments and faults according to Franklin's list of virtues on the charts at the end of chapters five through seventeen.

This daily process of evaluating his character began to take its toll. Franklin soon found his task more difficult than he had previously thought. He was discouraged at his shortcomings, humbled by his vices; but he did not give up. As he put it:

> While my care was employed in guarding against one fault, I was often surprised by another; habit took the advantage of inattention; inclination was sometimes too strong for reason. I concluded, at length, that the mere speculative conviction that it was our interest to be completely virtuous, was not sufficient to prevent our slipping; and that the contrary habits must be broken, and good ones acquired and established, before we can have dependence on a steady, uniform rectitude of conduct.[9]

Most can identify with Franklin's dilemma. He wanted to do right and live consistently by an agreeable set of virtues and principles. But like many of us, he found it more difficult than he had originally thought. However, the fact that he made the attempt, actually exhibiting these qualities — to a large degree — throughout the rest of his life, is evidence enough that we, too, can develop our character. Considering Benjamin Franklin's success and the lasting impact he made on history, we cannot ignore the importance of these qualities.

I believe his secret, in part, was *that the invisible is more important than the visible.* He chose to concentrate on and internalize invisible virtues until they became visible through his actions. It is from a display of whom one really is, that the visible symbols of success manifest themselves.

In the following chapters, we'll examine the thirteen character traits necessary for developing a virtuous, successful life that is free of regrets and full of accomplishments. If we prize, pursue and nurture these virtues until they become habits, we will never be the same. Neither will our country.

....

Questions for Thought

1. Would you describe Franklin as "successful"? Why or why not? Define "success."

2. Imagine that you are 89 years old and someone is writing an article about your life. What personal virtues, accomplishments and qualities would you most like them to identify?

3. List those virtues or qualities you would most like to see in yourself right now. What practical steps can you take to develop them?

THE CHARACTER REVOLUTION

PART TWO

The Face of Character

CHAPTER FIVE

Temperance

"Eat not to dullness, drink not to elevation."[1]

Everyone who knew the boy could see he was destined for greatness. He had a gift, a skill, a talent; he could play basketball with the best of them. Like all young stars, he dreamed of playing in the NBA. He realized early in life that to fulfill this dream he would have to live differently than those he saw "hanging in the streets." He would have to guard himself against the dangers his mother warned him about. His safety and success would depend upon exercising the virtue of self-control.

An exceptional athlete, this emerging talent trained hard at his sport; a habit he learned as a young boy and nurtured as a teenager. He knew better than to give in to peer pressure when it came to drugs and alcohol; he was determined to remain a disciplined player — to become the best he could be. And it paid off.

The talented young forward earned a basketball scholarship to the University of Maryland, home of one of America's most prestigious basketball programs. His future was bright. By his senior year, our young friend was named the number one college basketball player in the country, soon to be the Boston Celtics' first-draft pick. His name was Len Bias, and his self-control, self-discipline and sacrifice was about to pay off — until tragedy struck.

Shortly after being drafted by the Celtics, Len chose to "celebrate" with his buddies. Just this one time, he thought. What could it hurt? That night, Len made a choice. He let down his guard and decided to ignore the principles, values and rules he had learned as a child. After all, he reasoned, he was a grown man, a star athlete and an NBA player who could do what he wanted.

Len, like any of us, could indeed choose to do anything he wanted, but he, like us, could *not* choose the consequences. For this incredibly gifted and likable young man, the consequences were severe. For the first time, to anyone's knowledge, Len snorted cocaine. Surely his first time wouldn't be a big deal. Right?

Wrong! Within 48 hours of being the number two overall pick in the 1986 NBA draft, Len Bias was dead of cocaine poisoning. Sadly, an ordinarily disciplined young man had ignored the virtue that had sustained him and awarded him the opportunity to attend a nationally ranked university and play in the NBA — temperance.

Temperance is a not a common word these days. We rarely hear anyone telling us to exercise this virtue. In fact, we can hardly hear temperance's cry through the crowd of all-you-can-eat restaurants, two-for-one cocktail sales and nonstop amusement on television. Though advertisers would disagree, I'm convinced we should reinitiate temperance into our daily protocol.

With good reason, temperance was first on Franklin's list for virtuous living. To him, temperance meant: "Eat not to dullness, drink not to elevation." Franklin reasoned that temperance was "to procure that coolness and clearness of head, which is so necessary where constant vigilance was to be kept up, and guard maintained against the unremitting attraction of ancient habits, and force of perpetual temptations."[2]

If only able to "Just say no" to those things which prevent clearness of head, one could fight off unhealthy habits that negatively affect every area of life. Known to us today as moderation or self-restraint, temperance is an indispensable part of virtuous living. Why? Because failure to exercise self-control over our appetites or passions destroys us physically, mentally and emotionally — our guard goes down and the pull of ancient habits or perpetual temptations becomes too strong.

What we eat and drink, what we put into our bodies and how much we consume have a great impact on our potential. In short, how much we allow our passions to rule us determines our character and success.

Fall From Temperance

Before its fall, Rome was a prosperous, lawful, advanced society. People enjoyed enormous wealth, gorged on feasts and wine, and thrived on mindless entertainment. It was the world capital and pleasure was abundant. There was just one problem — people could never get enough.

Soon, darkness and mayhem became the norm. Roman officials knew their city was out of balance; residents were consuming more than farmers and merchants could produce. Bread was running out. Feeding the growing multitudes became increasingly difficult. Taxes had to be increased in order to subsidize the urban crowd, creating a growing resentment and anger in many citizens. Disaster was imminent.

> In short, how much we allow our passions to rule us determines our character and success.

In an effort to make the people happy, officials increased the level of entertainment in the Colosseum. The crowd, numbed by violence, attempted to satisfy their bloodlust by attending the gory gladiator games and chariot races. Contestants were literally sacrificed for the crowd's pleasure. The circus became the people's temple, but their thirst for satisfaction was never quenched; they wanted more, at greater and greater expense. Finally, at the onset of the sixth century, due to their own overindulgence, the city of Rome collapsed into ruins.[3]

We, too, are a society out of control. Fewer and fewer people are willing to sacrifice temporary pleasures for the sake of long-term gain. Like the Romans, it seems we Americans want more, better, bigger, and now. Daily, we are faced with countless choices concerning which products or services we want. These choices don't help our lives; they simply feed the deception that we need more to live better.

How wrong we are. Just consider how the lack of temperance has contributed to untold incidences of violence, theft, drunk-driving related accidents, unwanted pregnancies and broken marriages. Considering the health problems of overeating and drinking in our culture; the rise in related heart disease, cancer and drunk-driving deaths, each of us would do well to put temperance first on our personal list of virtues.

Alcohol, especially, has a numbing effect on our moral judgment. In freshman psychology, I was taught that when developing new habits, the "last learned is the first to go." Under the influence of alcohol, inhibitions, (especially newly acquired ones) are seriously compromised. We have all witnessed the sometimes radical differences in people's behavior under the influence of alcohol. Alcohol's ability to alter our mood and conscience has caused untold numbers of people to commit acts they would never have committed if sober. The cost in terms of human suffering is staggering.

This is why Franklin suggested temperance as the crucial virtue for successful living without regret. He implies that self-discipline is needed in every aspect of our life. The Webster New Encyclopedic Dictionary defines temperance as "moderation in action, thought, feeling, restraint; habitual moderation in the indulgence of the appetites or passions, especially moderation in or abstinence from the use of intoxicating drink."[4]

The Tempering Process

If we fail to rule our passions and refuse to live self-disciplined lives, disaster is imminent — just like it was in Rome. You see, some sort of "rule" is going to be imposed on all of us — one way or another. Voluntary self-rule is best. If, through self-restraint, we do what is right, we will enjoy the freedoms and benefits afforded those who live by proven principles, values and virtues. Otherwise, we can choose to live outside these natural and civil laws, risking the loss of our freedom and possibly our lives. Therefore, we must develop habits of temperance if we are to be highly effective people.

While working with "at-risk" students in schools throughout the country, it became evident to me that, if applied, this principle of temperance could dramatically change our society. Since many of these students were either ignorant of or unwilling to demonstrate adequate self-rule, those in authority, whether parent, school official or civil authority, had to impose rule over them. Had they fostered personal self-discipline, their lives and circumstances would have improved significantly. Rule, then, will come from within or it will come from without. But rule *will* be established.

Unfortunately, people like Len Bias remind us what lapses in self-rule can cost. Many end up hurting themselves severely through drug or alcohol abuse, promiscuity, crime or other activities that waste their God-given potential. Such undisciplined behavior puts a massive strain on our society. Consequently, how well we rule ourselves determines our true personal freedom and how well our society functions as a whole. It certainly determines our character!

Therefore, "eat not to dullness, drink not to elevation." Take the first step toward *restoring America's soul.*

> **Rule, then, will come from within or it will come from without. But rule *will* be established.**

Questions for Thought

1. Write a modern day definition of temperance. List at least five synonyms for temperance.

2. What does temperance, as Franklin describes it, have to do with developing your character?

3. What are some practical steps you could encourage others to take in developing a healthy, positive self-rule? In other words, what advice would you give to friends to nurture the virtue of temperance?

Instructions: This week, devote your energies to the virtue of Temperance. Try your hardest to avoid the slightest infraction against it, leaving the other virtues to their ordinary chance only marking every evening the faults of the day.

Temperance							
"Eat not to dullness, drink not to elevation."							
	SUN.	MON.	TUES.	WED.	THURS.	FRI.	SAT.
Temperance							
Silence							
Order							
Resolution							
Frugality							
Industry							
Sincerity							
Justice							
Moderation							
Cleanliness							
Tranquillity							
Chastity							
Humility							

CHAPTER SIX

Silence

"Speak not but what may benefit others or yourself; avoid trifling conversation."[1]

Franklin was convinced that if he could keep his head clear and his belly moderately content, he would be able to nurture all the other virtues on his list. He had a problem, though — he had a tough time keeping his mouth shut. That's why he was quick to put "silence" as the second essential trait for character development.

Here was a man driven by the pursuit of success, determined to do what it took to attain his goals and contribute to the young country in which he lived. To him, that meant learning as much as he could from those who were better versed in certain areas than he was. Since knowledge was obtained through listening rather than speaking, he reasoned that silence must be better than noise. Of silence he wrote: "Speak not but what may benefit others or yourself; avoid trifling conversation."

Silence is Golden

To speak only what is beneficial to one's self or others, or to avoid what we call "small talk" is a great challenge. Anyone who has ever tried this knows it's not easy. Words fly out of our mouths before we've given them much thought, often at great expense to the listeners and ourselves. Words hold the power of life and death. It is with words that revolutions are incited or forgotten, games won or lost, marriages strengthened or broken, talents encouraged or stifled and truths taught or mocked. They affect every area of our lives, either positively or negatively.

Let's face it: The tongue is a powerful tool that literally speaks volumes about who we are. Whatever we are on the inside, our beliefs, attitudes, feelings and emotions will all find their expression through our words. They can cause tremendous harm. Whereas, physical blows might bruise, verbal blows will scar. But under the control of a virtuous person, the tongue can be a wonderful tool that builds up, heals and gives hope, encouragement and life. As James the Elder stated: "If any one does not stumble in what he says, he is a perfect man."[2] A word aptly spoken, then, can build a student's self-esteem, heal a tense working relationship, foster hope in a discouraged neighbor, or bring life to a dream that once was thought dead.

> A word aptly spoken, then, can build a student's self-esteem, heal a tense working relationship, foster hope in a discouraged neighbor, or bring life to a dream that once was thought dead.

My friend Robert understood this well. I knew Robert from my college days at William and Mary in Virginia. I was on the football team so I'd often see him after practice or workouts. He was one of the hardest working men I had ever met and I valued his presence in my life. I was a struggling college student who could never quite figure out what I was doing with my life; he was a full-time janitor who always had a kind word or a ready ear.

Usually, I would hear Robert before I saw him. In his beautiful baritone voice, he would hum or sing down the hall, accompanied by the sound of a mop and bucket. I'd be studying in one of the rooms, poke my head out and watch this contented man as he worked his way toward me. His partially toothed smile would flash when he'd see me. He'd stop and lean on his mop, ready to listen.

I was not living a life of character and was often confused about what I should be doing. I had everything that most people considered necessary for happiness: friends, a good family, a good educational opportunity and an athletic scholarship. But still I wasn't happy. And my discontent usually spewed out of my mouth whenever Robert was around.

Maybe it was his confidence and peace that allowed me to trust him with my deepest thoughts. Maybe it was his willingness to stop what he was doing to hear me, or his deep joy that seemed always to radiate in his actions. Mostly, he knew when to speak (which wasn't much) and when to listen (which was often). I think that's what made me appreciate his friendship most.

Robert would often say to me: "The material things in life don't matter much. It's folks that count. If you wanna be happy, boy, you gotta do right by others and by God." Though his advice has long lingered with me, I don't remember Robert because of his eloquent language or his deep insights: rather, it was his contentment to say little and listen well that made the greatest impression on me.

Learning to Listen

Someone once said that God gave us two ears and one mouth that we might listen twice as much as we speak. Surely, Franklin had this in mind when he suggested we learn the value of silence.

But the noise all around us does not make this easy. Every office is humming with business machines and radios. Every mall has the buzz of hundreds of conversations and conflicts. Televisions are on continuously in many homes, telephones are ringing off the hook, traffic outside is roaring and neighbors are yelling. There is noise everywhere and silence certainly seems a luxury.

Quite intentionally, we must nurture an inward silence in our souls so we can successfully respond to the demands of our vocations and relationships. In other words, when we learn to be quiet on the inside, our chances for better listening increase. Listening well and saying little helps bring success without regret.

Unfortunately, most of us just aren't very good listeners. We need help. As one expert says: "Listening is the first learned communication skill, the most used, yet the least taught."[3] While our educational system pushes us to write well, read much and speak eloquently, we rarely have the benefit of formal instruction on listening skills. We think of listening as a natural phenomenon, not a learned ability. Our lack of listening skills costs a great deal.

Corporate executives estimate that listening errors are estimated to cost businesses upward of $1 billion a year. Not long ago, the International Listening Association reported that at least three million divorces in the U.S. are related to an inability — or an unwillingness — of one or both parties to listen and care about the spoken views and needs of their spouse. Other communication professionals say that the principle cause behind the sinking of the ocean liner Titanic, the disastrous Charge of the Light Brigade, as well as the enormous loss of human life at the Battle of Gettysburg can be traced to listening errors and garbled messages. More recently, at least a dozen airplane crashes have been attributed to poor listening skills, and many employers say they refuse to hire anyone who cannot listen, regardless of how good their résumé is.[4]

Franklin was on to something. Listening well and saying little helps us gain wisdom and knowledge we would otherwise miss out on. But how do we develop such skills? A simple checklist of listening for success will help:

- concentrate on the speaker
- don't interrupt or get distracted
- focus your thoughts
- turn off inward "noise" and tune out the outward noise
- develop empathy
- be patient
- seek clarification by asking questions
- don't be intent on hearing yourself talk
- don't spend the whole time framing your response

Let others have their say, listen to them with concentration, and speak only after you've thought through an answer. These are simple steps, but ones that surely will take us a long way.

Finally, we would all do well to remember this startling truth: "It is in their listening that people are most easily persuaded." The author of that piece of advice should know: Adolph Hitler was able to convince thousands of people to commit atrocities because they failed to listen with discernment. With our increased ability to listen well, we will need to think deeply about what is being spoken. When we don't listen with thought, we are easily misled.

....

Questions for Thought

1. Franklin reasoned that since knowledge is obtained through hearing rather than talking, silence must be better than speaking. How can you gain knowledge through silence?

2. How do words reflect who we are? Which five words best reflect who you are?

3. Personal challenge: See if you can go an entire week without once having to ask anyone to repeat themselves, concentrating greatly on what's being said while trying to improve your listening skills.

Instructions: This week, devote your energies to the virtue of Silence. Try your hardest to avoid the slightest infraction against it, leaving the other virtues to their ordinary chance only marking every evening the faults of the day.

Silence							
"Speak not but what may benefit others or yourself; avoid trifling conversation."							
	SUN.	MON.	TUES.	WED.	THURS.	FRI.	SAT.
Temperance							
Silence							
Order							
Resolution							
Frugality							
Industry							
Sincerity							
Justice							
Moderation							
Cleanliness							
Tranquillity							
Chastity							
Humility							

CHAPTER SEVEN

Order

"Let all your things have their place; let each part of your business have its time."[1]

Not long ago, I met a man — I'll call him Ron — whom I came to respect a great deal. Our wives had gone to college together and, though I wasn't close friends with Ron, I could tell he was a man of character: honest, virtuous and hardworking.

He worked full-time at an inner-city mission helping people in poverty find jobs. At night and on weekends, Ron went to graduate school to complete his second master's degree. He was an active leader in his church and the new father of a little girl. He even managed to work a part-time job for extra income, so his wife could care full-time for their baby. Ron seemed energized by the demands of his full schedule; instead of growing tired, he only seemed to grow stronger.

For several years, Ron's pace stayed the same. He was always busy, but he was always smiling. Whenever I'd see him, he'd talk enthusiastically about his studies or about a low-income father he had helped land a well-paying job. When I'd ask him about his family, he'd confidently respond, "Fine, fine. We're all fine."

But everything wasn't fine. One day the demands on his time

took their toll, and Ron snapped. He lost his temper, stole some money from his employer and left town, alone. For the next six months, Ron hid from his friends, the police and even his family. His life had spun out of control, and he no longer knew how to respond.

That was six years ago. Today, Ron is slowly rebuilding his life. Thankfully, he is reunited with his wife and child, has made restitution with his boss and is thinking about school again. But Ron will never again be the same. And in some ways, that's a very good thing.

Putting Our Lives in Order

Unfortunately, Ron learned the hard way what a life of unrealistic demands can do to a person. He was going in so many different directions that he was unable to sustain any order or peace in his life. The chaos of busyness and the tyranny of urgency got the best of Ron — something had to give.

> Franklin believed that well-arranged time is a sure mark of a well-arranged mind.

Today, Ron has learned to slow down, to prioritize and to put his life in order. If things get too harried, he will pause and re-focus his attention on what matters most to him. It is a valuable lesson, especially when contemporary life can seem so rushed.

Benjamin Franklin understood this basic principle which we call time management. That's why he placed "order" as the third virtue on his list. He wrote: "Let all your things have their place; let each part of your business have its time." Such prioritizing of his time could, at least in theory, allow Franklin "more time for project and study."

In other words, Franklin believed that well-arranged time is a sure mark of a well-arranged mind. If a person could order his life in terms of what was most important and stay consistent with and committed to that schedule, he would surely experience success without regrets. In fact, it's quite possible Franklin conjured up an early version of our modern Day-Timer — he wanted desperately to get his schedule on paper so as not to be easily distracted.[2]

But this was no easy task for the multi-talented revolutionary.

Organizing his life was nothing short of a miracle. He had so many interests, business ventures, relationships and projects going at the same time that he was perpetually struggling to manage his time wisely and effectively.

After his great experiment of living a virtuous life, he wrote:

> Order too, with regard to places for things, papers, etc., I found extremely difficult to acquire. I had not been early accustomed to it, and having an exceeding good memory, I was not so sensible of the inconvenience attending want of method. This article (of writing down his schedule) therefore cost me so much painful attention and my faults in it vexed me so much, and I made so little progress in amendment, and had such frequent relapses, that I was almost ready to give up the attempt, and content myself with a faulty character in that respect.[3]

In other words, a lack of restraint in keeping an orderly schedule almost pushed Franklin over the edge. Inability to follow his "Day-Timer" revealed his vice in this area. The schedule, instead of helping him, became a source of frustration. It was too easy to get distracted with inappropriate temptations and, in the process, settle for less than the best.

In his autobiography, he likened his struggle to the following story:

> I was almost ready to give up the attempt, and content myself with a faulty character in that respect, like the man who, in buying an ax of a Smith desired to have the whole of its surface as bright as the edge. The Smith consented to grind it bright for him if he would turn the wheel; he turned, while the Smith pressed the broad face of the ax hard and heavily on the stone, which made the turning of it very fatiguing. The man came every now and then from the wheel to see how the work went on, and at length would take his ax as it was, without farther grinding. "No," said the Smith, "turn on, turn on; we shall have it bright by-and-by; as yet, it is

only speckled." "Yes," says the man, "but I think I like a speckled ax best."[4]

Eliminating the Speckles

Unfortunately, there are numerous "speckled areas" in my life and probably in yours, too. It is easy to get trapped in the whirlwind of daily living, settling for less than the best; but if we keep our eye on *progress* and not *perfection,* staying committed to our priorities one day at a time, I believe we can eliminate this sense of chaos. Should we fail to meet our daily goals, we can learn from our errors to improve the next day. Failure can be a powerful teacher — one that doesn't have to keep us from trying again.

> Failure can be a powerful teacher—one that doesn't have to keep us from trying again.

Such a commitment to order, or what the dictionary defines as "the arrangement or sequence of objects in position or of events in time" will always bring good results.[5] Here the old agricultural law of sowing and reaping directly applies. If we sow seeds of good investments in our schedule (i.e., spend meaningful time with our families, study for our personal enjoyment as well as our careers, relax with friends, improve our talents), we are sure to reap significant rewards: peace, joy and fulfillment to name just a few. As John Wanamaker said: "People who cannot find time for recreation are obliged sooner or later to find time for illness."[6]

How many times have we heard from friends that if they had their lives to live over, they would spend more time with loved ones and less time working? Though many have experienced worldly success, how much of it came with a fair amount of regrets?

Robert Shapiro, the famous lawyer for O.J. Simpson in what has been viewed as the trial of the century, is living proof. The case demanded two years of extremely intense time and energy. Just months after the verdict, Shapiro was asked on prime time television what he would do if O.J. came to him again. Would he take the case again? Would he do it all over? Without hesitation, he answered, "Professionally, it was an opportunity I would never have missed. Personally, it was at great expense to my family, and I would never want to do it again. I missed out on some of my children's most important times."

A week later, *Time* magazine asked Shapiro if he regretted taking the case at all. "Well, it's not an experience I would want to duplicate, but it's not a case I would have missed. In terms of emotional strain on my wife and children, the constant scrutiny, the false rumors and the overall commitment to spend sixteen months of your life on one case, the cost to my family was inordinate. From a professional point of view, I'm very proud of what I did."

Obviously, Shapiro's success came with some regrets, regrets he can never undo. Sure, he will forever be known for his role in the infamous trial. But it cost him and his family dearly.

When we learn to develop our personal character by ordering our lives, we can have success without regrets. We can take charge of the time we've been given, even though we live in a society of over-stimulation — a world that often seems out of control. We must not let a crisis, what seems like the trial of the century, distract us from what is most important. We must take to heart the adage: "To become a man of the hour, we must learn first to make every minute count." Ordering our lives is a virtue we cannot afford to ignore.

....

Questions for Thought

1. Can you remember a time you felt like you were going in too many different directions, unable to sustain any order or peace in your life? What happened?

2. How is the old agricultural law of sowing and reaping good advice for ordering our schedules and managing our time?

3. "To become a man of the hour, we must learn first to make every minute count." What goals do you hope to accomplish for the upcoming year? How can you make every minute count in achieving them without letting your life get out of control?

Instructions: This week, devote your energies to the virtue of Order. Try your hardest to avoid the slightest infraction against it, leaving the other virtues to their ordinary chance only marking every evening the faults of the day.

Order							
"Let all your things have their place; let each part of your business have its time."							
	SUN.	MON.	TUES.	WED.	THURS.	FRI.	SAT.
Temperance							
Silence							
Order							
Resolution							
Frugality							
Industry							
Sincerity							
Justice							
Moderation							
Cleanliness							
Tranquillity							
Chastity							
Humility							

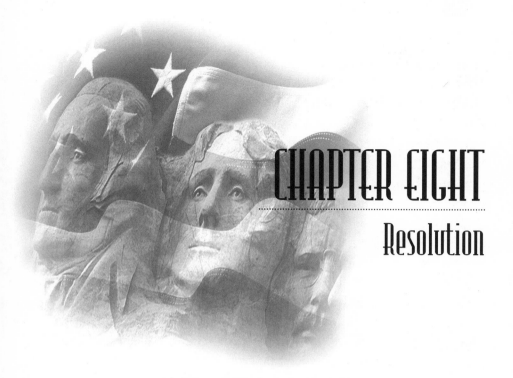

CHAPTER EIGHT

Resolution

"Resolve to perform what you ought; perform without fail
what you resolve."[1]

He was a bad boy. It was the 1850s, and children were not supposed to be bad. The teachers said he talked too much, asked too many questions and was easily distracted by other things. He would read books he wasn't assigned and draw pictures that weren't at all like they were supposed to be. No amount of discipline could change the young boy's behavior or get his attention. Finally, after just a few months of formal schooling, his teachers had endured enough of the boy's disobedience. They asked his mother to come in for a meeting.

"We have watched your son for three months now. We have tried everything to make him fit into our system. But it has not worked," they told the silent, tiny mother. She listened, her heart aching for her child. "We are sorry," the teachers told her, "but we have determined that your son is not educable and probably will never be able to learn." At that point, the young mother gripped her son's hand proudly, stared at the teachers, and after a long, uncomfortable pause, simply said, "Fine. I shall educate him myself." And she did.[2]

For the next ten years, the mother taught her son at their New York home. They read books together, solved math problems, and studied nature, science and history. When she saw that her son had a particular interest in science, they performed fun experiments or built science projects. The mother was determined to prove to those teachers that her son was "educable." She resolved to pour herself into her child, knowing all along that he could learn. His biggest problem, she reasoned, was that he was smarter than most children.

By the time the boy was twelve, he went to work as a newsboy on the railroad. Later, he worked as a telegraph operator and invented a receiver and transmitter. Throughout his lifetime, he patented over thirteen hundred inventions, including the phonograph, the microphone and the incandescent electric lamp. He ran the first centralized electric-light power plant in the world, invented the Kinescope and developed talking motion pictures. It is the "uneducable" Thomas Edison who recognized that genius is "two percent inspiration and ninety-eight percent perspiration."[3] No doubt he made his mother proud.

Thomas Edison learned early on never to quit. His mother showed him selfless resolution and fierce tenacity by educating her son at home. In spite of what others said, he learned a great deal and became a student for life. Consequently, his incredible determination as an inventor literally changed the world. And we have plenty of reasons to thank Mrs. Edison for her unwavering confidence in her son. Can you imagine a world without electric lights, telephones or movies?!

The Fruit of Resolve

Likewise, Ben Franklin was no stranger himself to resolution. With his countless experiments and inventions, his prolific writing and printing projects, his untiring contributions to statesmanship and governmental development, Franklin knew the importance of perseverance. He had to, or none of his incredible endeavors would have been achieved. Just think of it. If he had not followed through on his commitments, Americans would not have had local libraries, *Poor*

Richard's Almanacs, lightening rods, bifocal spectacles, and, of course, the famous Franklin signature on Declaration of Independence.

So, on his list of virtues for character development, Franklin placed "resolution" as number four: "Resolve to perform what you ought; perform without fail what you resolve." Implied in his simple formula for getting tasks done is a determination and integrity many of us find lacking in our everyday lives.

"Resolve to perform what you ought" means we must first be able to recognize the right thing to do. It is no accident that Franklin placed resolution after the virtue of order. When we determine and order our priorities, we must then resolve to keep them. In other words, we must learn to follow through on our commitments, even when it is inconvenient.

Sadly, this sense of "doing the right thing" and keeping our word has been lost in our culture of creature comforts, selfishness and independence. We hear advice like: If your marriage isn't making you happy, never mind the vows you took; leave your spouse and children so you can finally be "all you can be." If a job isn't exactly what you thought it would be, never mind that you signed a contract; quit immediately because you deserve more. If your team or club is not achieving what you wanted, never mind that you gave your word to participate; drop out and find another team.

> We must learn to follow through on our commitments, even when it is inconvenient.

No wonder the United States has the highest divorce rate in the world. At the present rate, approximately half of all marriages can be expected to end in divorce, according to the U.S. Department of Health and Human Services.[4] No wonder the number of temporary employment agencies has doubled in the last twenty years. And no wonder _The Washington Post_ recently reported that the average teenager spends only 1.8 hours per week reading, 5.6 hours per week on homework, and an average of 21 hours per week doing the easiest thing possible: watching television.[5] Ours is a nation of instant gratification and many, many paths of least resistance.

Let's face it: Americans today want a life that is easy, comfortable and immediate. Most of us don't like waiting in line; we want fast food now. We will consider cheating or lying to get our way. Hard work, integrity and long-term commitments to doing what's right are difficult to come by. But as Harvard law professor, Stephen Carter, recently said in his excellent book, *Integrity:* "America's integrity dilemma [is this]: we are all full of fine talk about how desperately our society needs it, but when push comes to shove, we would just as soon be on the winning side . . . Integrity is like the weather: everybody talks about it but nobody knows what to do about it."[6]

But Franklin knew. His life proved his sense of integrity and resolve. America is the great country it is, largely because women and men of every generation resolved to work hard, keeping their commitments to that which they believed in. They, like Edison and Franklin, knew what it meant to "Perform without fail what you resolve." In turn, they experienced authentic personal successes that were beneficial to entire communities.

There was even a time in our country when a person's word was as good as any written contract. In fact, your word was your line of credit. If you told the local grocer you would pay him later for his food, the grocer had no reason to doubt you. Can you imagine today going to Sears or Safeway and telling the clerk you'd pay him next week?!

Press On

Franklin knew what it was to desire a particular thing and make a plan to acquire it — and our country is the better for it. But he also knew that we have a tendency to get intellectually and emotionally excited for a short period of time only to see the excitement wane before attaining results. That's why we've got to be willing to press on in attaining our goals, to be faithful with both big and small commitments, to make good on our word and to resolve never to give up.

When we do press on, the rewards and feeling of accomplishment far outweigh the necessary struggles involved. Most likely, our resolve will change our world. That's why we must remember that Thomas Edison worked on about 18,000 experiments before he perfected the arc light. Dr. Jonas Salk worked sixteen hours a day for three years to perfect the polio vaccine.[7] While he was in a concentration camp in Russia, serving time for denouncing the socialist leader, Stalin, Aleksandr Solzhenitsyn composed an entire novel in his head. He wrote it down only after he got out of prison. In North America, just before the Civil War, Harriet Tubman risked her life hundreds of times by helping slaves gain their freedom.[8]

The list goes on and on because, as Samuel Johnson said: "Great works are performed, not by strength but by perseverance." That's why it's so important to "resolve to perform what you ought; perform without fail what you resolve."

Questions for Thought

1. Why do you think Franklin placed resolution right after order on his list of virtues?

2. What are some commitments your generation has made (or needs to make) in order to restore America to greatness?

3. How can Samuel Johnson's statement, "Great works are performed, not by strength but by perseverance," apply to your life right now?

Instructions: This week, devote your energies to the virtue of Resolution. Try your hardest to avoid the slightest infraction against it, leaving the other virtues to their ordinary chance only marking every evening the faults of the day.

Resolution							
"Resolve to perform what you ought; perform without fail what you resolve."							
	SUN.	MON.	TUES.	WED.	THURS.	FRI.	SAT.
Temperance							
Silence							
Order							
Resolution							
Frugality							
Industry							
Sincerity							
Justice							
Moderation							
Cleanliness							
Tranquillity							
Chastity							
Humility							

CHAPTER NINE

Frugality

"Make no expense but to do good to others or yourself;
waste nothing."[1]

The table was set for the four of us. We were waiting for Dad to get home from work, only we all knew there was not much work to be found. My father had been laid off from Virginia Electric & Power Company so money was tight. Dinner proved it. Every night we had potatoes cooked in every imaginable form, in every imaginable way: mashed, home fried, French fried, scalloped, casseroled, baked, even shaped into what was supposed to be "meat loaf." When my sister and I complained, Mama just explained that we had to get the most for the little bit we had — potatoes were cheap.

"If you don't like it," she exclaimed, "there's plenty of grass out back!" Remarkably, I learned to love those potatoes. I didn't know it at the time, but I was also learning from my parents, on a small scale, the lessons they had learned during the Great Depression of the 1930s. That is, we must get the most out of what resources we have. We must make wise use of our money and learn the benefits of delayed gratification.

They even taught me how to pay my own way. I remember wanting to cut grass to earn money, but the family lawn mower was too dilapidated to endure five or six lawns a week. So, my dad loaned me $60 to buy a new mower. Every week after working, I would place nearly all my money into an old pickle jar that served as my "savings bank." Finally, after four weeks, I was able to pay back my father. By the age of twelve, I was financially independent!

But as the saying goes, that was then, this is now. Not many of us today know what it means to save money in old pickle jars. Many of us have developed the attitude that we should be able to buy what we want, when we want it, because we "deserve" it. We don't think through how we will pay for it later. Money machines, instant loans, computer banking and credit cards make spending beyond our means enticing and expected. Let's face it, most of us know too well the reality of the saying, "Money talks — and all mine says is good-bye!"

Maybe it's no accident, then, that Franklin put "frugality" next on his list of virtues. He knew that one's view of money is *directly linked* to the commitments and resolutions one makes. His idea of frugality was simple: "Make no expense but to do good to others or yourself; waste nothing." In other words, Franklin was concerned about going into financial debt, believing it would actually keep him from producing "affluence and independence."[2]

Instead, he said, we should "waste nothing," keeping ourselves free from the oppression of debts, making "more easy the practice of sincerity and justice."[3] Franklin knew that those who are financially free are seldom anxious, are more easily content, earn more and give generously. They know how to manage their money so they are able to focus their energy on things of more importance. Good thought. Yet, how in the world can Franklin's advice apply to people today?

Going, Going, Gone

Indebtedness is a crippling epidemic in our culture. One journalist recently wrote: "As a nation, we save less than two percent of our income. We write over one million bad checks every day. Consumer debt sits like an invisible elephant in the center of far too many homes."[4] That's not all. Governmental spending rose five-fold between 1960 and 1990. I believe the congressional national debt is merely a reflection of a society gone economically awry — an extension of what we do individually.

How we use our money indicates what we value most in our society. We value entertainment more than education: professional athletes and entertainers are paid large sums of money while our nation's educators struggle to provide for themselves and their families. Advertisers imply that lotteries or their various products are the answer to our problems. Authentic needs are blown out of proportion and frivolities become greedy "wants." In short, we live in a culture that still thinks you can buy happiness.

I don't know many people who aren't struggling to earn more so they can have more. Credit cards are often randomly issued to young college students — most of whom have never been taught how to manage their money — so they can "build credit." Meanwhile, they end up spending money they don't have and acquiring debt they won't want. In fact, our society teaches us that as we grow older, our "needs" grow with us. It seems natural to invest each raise we get on ourselves: a new stereo, a nice deck on our house, a luxury car. If we live "normal" lives in American culture, it is presupposed that we will naturally accumulate more for our comfortable lifestyles. And we will never have enough. The great American Dream has become a nightmare!

> We live in a culture that still thinks you can buy happiness.

Money concerns cause a tremendous strain on families and marriages. How many children have been sacrificed on the altar of materialism? How many marriages have ended because of financial tensions? We borrow more money for this or that and become slaves to the lender. And if you don't think debt is a hard taskmaster, try missing a few payments. Indeed, our consumer-driven, materialistic society makes daily money matters tough to deal with. But it doesn't have to be that way.

Breaking Free

Franklin's advice to "Make no expense but to do good to others or yourself" is as relevant today for creating success without regrets as any good financial tip.

But what does money have to do with character development? Plenty. Consider all the times a businessman is tempted to fudge a little on his tax reports. Consider how higher salaries dictate choices, regardless of personal satisfaction or the cost to one's family. Consider how greed has created many a scandal in the political and economic worlds.

If we spent more time prioritizing the things in life that really matter and less time worrying about our finances, we could break ourselves free from the trap so many of us feel caught in. Even when money increases, it is foolish to set our hopes on it. Why? Because life does not consist of material things. What would you give for your eyesight? If you were blind, would you pay any price to see? If it cost you every material possession you had to save your child, would you give it all? Of course!

> It matters very little how much you make; what matters, is how well you manage it.

Money is important but not *that* important. It is simply a tool to be used wisely for the benefit of others and ourselves. Of course it won't benefit anyone if you can't control it or you have to keep giving it to bankers, department stores, car dealerships, etc. It matters very little how much you make; what matters, is how well you manage it.

A workshop leader teaching money management asked his class: "Have you ever heard people say, 'I just don't know where my money goes?' " When many in the class smiled and nodded, he added, "We don't know because we don't look. We don't look because we don't want to know."[5] Possibly you are now ready to take a look. If you find yourself in debt today, or if you're interested in knowing how to become more financially fit, pay close attention to this advice given by an old camel trader and a young man from Babylon.

Lessons From Babylon

In his classic, *The Richest Man In Babylon,* George S. Clason writes parables about personal finance. The book is rooted upon the adage that "A lean purse is easier to cure than to endure."

For those who find themselves in debt, Clason offers the parable of a humble camel trader named Dabasir. Dabasir found himself enslaved to debt, discovering painfully that a person enslaved to debt also loses the soul of a free man. Fortunately for Dabasir, he eventually discovered a way to set himself free. He wrote his plan down on five clay tablets which were excavated thousands of years later by a professor Caldwell, then translated by professor Shrewsbury — a man in a great deal of debt himself. Shrewsbury found, that through determined application of the camel trader's plan to his own situation, he too was able to become a free man. What is this plan that is as successful in modern times as it was in ancient times? It is quite simple. Dabasir determined to save ten percent of his income, live on seventy percent, and pay off his creditors with the remaining twenty percent.

> Yet, to those willing to sacrifice immediate gratification—in the interest of gaining life-long freedom—the struggle will prove invaluable.

You may look at those percentages and find that they are not reasonable for your situation. The key to regaining the soul of a free man lay not so much in the percentages, but in the consistent application to the plan. When you are trapped there is a great deal of struggle necessary to free yourself. This struggle requires the virtues of frugality, resolve, moderation, industry and order. Yet, to those willing to sacrifice immediate gratification — in the interest of gaining life long freedom — the struggle will prove invaluable. Once you are out of debt you can apply the "Seven Cures for a Lean Purse."

The "Seven Cures for a Lean Purse" is a story describing a financial plan — a plan which enables individuals to become financially secure. The story begins with two friends struggling to understand why they're unable to accumulate any wealth, even though they're rd. The two lament that they simply live from week never get ahead. Their frustrations lead them to uildhood friend Arkad — who has become the rich- .., ..)n — to inquire of his secret for gaining wealth.

Arkad informs his friends: "If you have not acquired more than a bare existence in the years since we were youths, it is either because you have failed to learn the laws that govern the building of wealth, or you do not observe them." Arkad further revealed that to obtain great wealth two things were required: time and study. He told his friends he had begun accumulating wealth when he recognized that, ". . . a part of all I earned was mine to keep." Arkad realized he had paid the baker, the tailor and the banker, but he had never paid himself. Every month Arkad determined to pay himself ten percent of his income, living off the remaining ninety percent. It was this ten-percent that cured his empty purse and eventually led to his great wealth. Arkad was so successful that the King approached him to teach others his "cure." With one hundred teachers gathered in the Temple of Learning, Arkad taught the seven cures for a lean purse.

The First Cure - Start thy purse to fattening:

"For every ten coins thou placest within thy purse take for use but nine. Thy purse will start to fatten at once and its increased weight will feel good in thy hand and bring satisfaction to thy soul." Arkad concluded his first lesson by asking his students which they desired most: daily gratification or substantial belongings? If you take the coins out for the first, you will not acquire the second.

The Second Cure - Control thy expenditures:

Preparing and following a budget is the focus of this second cure. If we fail to budget our expenses, then Arkad correctly states; "That which each of us calls our 'necessary expenses' will always grow equal to our income unless we protest to the contrary." We need to set limits — or reduce our lifestyle — if we want our purse to fatten.

The Third Cure - Make thy gold multiply:

"Put each coin to laboring that it may reproduce its kind even as the flocks of the field and help bring to thee income, a stream of wealth that shall flow constantly into thy purse." Making wise, *consistent* investments over *time* produces the miracle of compound interest we have all heard about. Get your ten percent working for you; then, even while you are resting, your gold is working.

The Fourth Cure - Guard thy treasures from loss:

"Guard thy treasures from loss by investing only where thy principal is safe; where it may be reclaimed if desirable; and where thou will not fail to collect a fair rental. Consult with wise men. Secure advice of those experienced in the profitable handling of gold. Let their wisdom protect thy treasure from unsafe investments." Investing wisely and not speculatively will provide "security for thy principle." Obviously if we want our money to work for us we must protect it against loss. That's why study and caution are necessary for a steady stream of gold.

The Fifth Cure - Make of thy dwelling a profitable investment:

By using part of the nine-tenths you live on to buy an appreciable investment — your home — you help your gold grow more rapidly. Besides the obvious tax advantages, this is another way to pay yourself, even as you pay the lender. If your income increases, make an additional monthly payment each year. It will save you tens of thousands of dollars in interest; so, as soon as possible, "Own thy own home."

The Sixth Cure - Insure a future income:

"Provide in advance for the needs of thy growing age and the protection of thy family." In this cure, Arkad clearly states the purpose for faithfully saving and investing your gold. Hope for the best, but prepare for the worst.

The Seventh Cure - Increase thy ability to earn:

"Cultivate thy own powers, to study and become wiser, to become more skillful, to so act as to respect thyself." If ever there was a time when we needed to heed this advice, it is now. To survive and thrive in this dynamic global economy, we must be dedicated to life-long learning. It is essential, in today's marketplace, that we demonstrate creativity and flexibility, all the while regularly sharpening our skills.

We would do well to learn these valuable lessons. But learning is not enough, we must act!

It Can Be Done

Consider the wonderful example of eighty-seven-year-old Oseola McCarty. She surprised the nation by donating $150,000 to the University of Southern Mississippi to establish a scholarship fund for black students. The school often receives donations of this size, so what was the big deal? Incredibly, Miss McCarty earned the money from washing clothes for local residents over a period of seventy-five years. Instead of owning a big house or buying new clothes, she saved her money because she just wanted to "help black kids get an education."

Her gift generated a nationwide response of over $33,000 in additional contributions; her charity even sparked a letter from President Clinton for her "unselfish deed — a remarkable example of the spirit and ingenuity that made America great."

"I'm glad I paid my donation to them," said the laundry woman who claimed her only education came from the Bible. "If I had any more, I'd give it to them, too."[6] She knew the secret to living well: Happiness is not contained in what you own, but in what you give.

This is the attitude we ought to have when developing the quality of frugality. The word frugal actually comes from the Latin word frugalis, which means "virtuous, having self-restraint, being thrifty, bearing fruit; of value."[7] The individual who is frugal, then, like Miss McCarty, is "characterized by displaying or reflecting economy in the use of resources."[8] To be frugal is to be so concerned about doing good with our resources that we escape the bondage and deception of money. It is to waste nothing, not our finances, our talents nor our opportunities to invest in the things that matter most.

People who live by the principles of financial freedom know the benefits of wise spending, rich giving and contented living. What happens as a result? Their rewards are out of this world!

....

Questions for Thought

1. Those who are free from the worries of debt and financial pressures generally have what kind of qualities or character traits?

2. Given our unique set of contemporary financial woes, how in the world can Franklin's advice on frugality apply to people today?

3. What do you think the difference between "need" and "want" is?

Instructions: This week, devote your energies to the virtue of Frugality. Try your hardest to avoid the slightest infraction against it, leaving the other virtues to their ordinary chance only marking every evening the faults of the day.

Frugality							
"Make no expense but to do good to others or yourself; waste nothing."							
	SUN.	MON.	TUES.	WED.	THURS.	FRI.	SAT.
Temperance							
Silence							
Order							
Resolution							
Frugality							
Industry							
Sincerity							
Justice							
Moderation							
Cleanliness							
Tranquillity							
Chastity							
Humility							

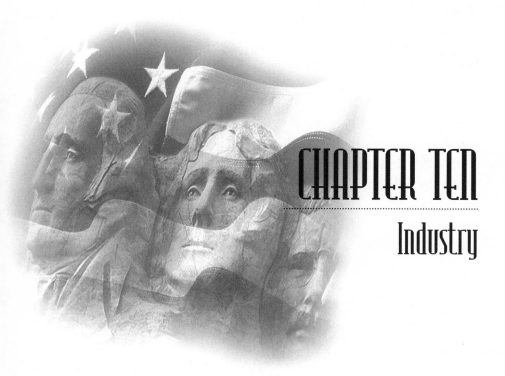

CHAPTER TEN

Industry

"Lose no time; be always employed in something useful;
cut off all unnecessary actions."[1]

When our country started to move away from being an agricultural society in the late 1800s, our sense of work quite naturally began to change. The Industrial Revolution ushered in a whole new way of looking at life: new gadgets, urbanization and machinery made life easier for most Americans. Cars, electricity, refrigeration, telephones, sewing machines and the like all began to create a lifestyle of convenience. As a result, I don't have any "cow-milking-in-the-snow" stories to relate like my parents did, but I, for one, am particularly thankful I can keep bottled milk in the refrigerator right in my own home!

In the same way, technology brings a new level of convenience to our generation. We can e-mail, fax, voice mail and computerize. Nearly everything we do in our professional and personal lives is changing. Children are entertained by video games, teenagers listen to CD Walkmans or watch MTV; mothers pop dinners into microwaves, while dads surf the Internet for the latest investment tips. We have become a nation that barely has to lift a finger to perform the most basic daily tasks.

Somewhere along the way, we lost our sense of balance. Some have become workaholics, deriving their self-worth from performance on the job. They believe the more they work the more valuable they are. Others have all but forgotten the dignity derived from hard work and a job well done. Today's work ethic reflects many other declining attitudes; if the work's too hard, quit; do as little work as possible and get paid as much for it as you can. Commitment to getting a task done is growing increasingly rare; commitment to doing it right is rarer still.

We need the dignity of hard work to develop in us a sense of contribution and accomplishment. As Will Rogers put it: "What the country needs is dirtier fingernails and cleaner minds."[2] Perhaps that is why Franklin placed "industry" right next to frugality on his list; he knew that the more diligently and efficiently we worked, the better our chances to reap economic and personal rewards.

> "What the country needs is dirtier fingernails and cleaner minds."

Hi Ho, Hi Ho

Franklin defined industry in the following way: "Lose no time; be always employed in something useful; cut off all unnecessary actions." Each aspect of this virtue ensures dignity of work — an essential quality for living well without regrets.

The picture Fyodor Dostoyevski described in his book, *The House of the Dead,* best illustrates this need for purposeful, significant work. In a prison setting, the Russian writer described life for the inmates: "If he had to move a heap of earth from one place to another and back again — I believe the convict would hang himself . . . preferring rather to die than endure such humiliation, shame, and torture."[3] Deprived of *meaningful* work, Dostoyevski believed men and women would lose their reason for existence, causing them to go stark raving mad. Franklin's simple formula, "Lose no time; be always employed in something useful; cut off all unnecessary actions," could help revolutionize our personal character and professional careers.

First, Franklin said, "lose no time." This encourages us in the same way as the popular Latin saying, "Carpe diem" or "Seize the day." When we make the most of each opportunity we're given, when we don't allow time to slip by and we don't sit in idleness, our work and our lives become meaningful to us personally and beneficial to those around us.

Certainly, Franklin was not suggesting we become workaholics — regardless of the cost to our families or ourselves — or define our personal identity by what we do. No, this advice, not to lose time, is different. Franklin urges us to view opportunities and priorities as both responsibilities and privileges. We must learn to pay attention to the little things in our jobs that prepare us for bigger things in the future. So, rather than being motivated by a paycheck, our work should be motivated by an attitude of enjoyment and purpose.

I think Charles Kingsley had the right idea when he wrote:

> Thank God every morning when you get up that you have something to do that day which must be done, whether you like it or not. Being forced to work, and forced to do your best, will breed in you temperance and self-control, diligence and strength of will, cheerfulness and content, and a hundred virtues which the idle never know.[4]

Worthy Investments

That brings us to the second part of Franklin's formula for industry: "Be always employed in something useful." Whether we like our job or dream of doing something else, we can always find something useful — something worth investing our time and talents into — wherever we are. Everyone benefits if we look for opportunities to contribute to others and if we search for ways to make our communities better.

This attitude seems almost antithetical in our current age of manipulation and greed. I'll never forget a job I had in college, working in a factory to help pay for school. Since I was taught at home to give "an honest day's work for an honest day's pay," I knew I was expected do my best, even if I was just moving cartons and crates around a warehouse.

I was convinced that even though I was working for someone else's company, I was actually "self-employed." Why? Because if I failed to do my job properly, I knew I would soon be woefully unemployed!

Unfortunately, my foreman didn't have the same expectations. For instance, sometimes when I'd finish my work, since I was still on the clock I'd ask for more. Yet, my foreman and some other employees actually told me on several occasions to stop working so hard. Their intent was to work as little as possible for as much money as possible. Some of the older workers wanted me to slow down because I was showing them up!

> An individual does not have to earn a great salary in order to contribute great things to the community!

Hiding out on a factory roof — because I completed an eight-hour work assignment in five hours — provided very little dignity. So after a few months, I moved on. Even though the money was great, I knew enough to recognize an unhealthy situation.

Restoring Dignity

Work, in our country, is too often viewed as an evil burden we must bear in order to survive. But it doesn't have to be. We must remember: There is dignity in all work — not just those intellectual pursuits, corporate careers or entertainment jobs that seem glamorous and enticing. People who are working hard, gainfully employed, and creating beauty, might not receive the same remuneration as someone else, but their work reflects a dignity all its own. Their contribution is just as important and valuable to the health of the whole community as it is to their own personal growth. An individual does not have to earn a great salary in order to contribute great things to the community!

With this in mind, the third part of Franklin's formula is simple enough: "Cut off all unnecessary actions." We need to spend more time on the tasks we know we're supposed to be doing and less time on busy work. And we mustn't lose sight of the value of our own work by comparing ourselves, or our careers, to others. Character, commitment and discipline are required to perform any job that is to be done well. Therefore, true satisfaction lies in providing a full day's work for a full day's pay.

The virtue of industry and the advice to "lose no time; be always employed in something useful; cut off all unnecessary actions" is vital to our sense of work, contribution and accomplishment. Dr. Martin Luther King, Jr., a man who worked tirelessly for the good of our nation, who knew the joy and dignity of his calling, best reflected this attitude and virtue in his life. I have always loved how eloquently he defined his philosophy of industry. May it be ours as well.

> Whatever your life's work is, do it well. Even if it does not fall in the category of one of the so-called big professions, do it well. If it falls your lot to be a street sweeper, sweep streets like Michelangelo painted pictures, like Shakespeare wrote poetry, like Beethoven composed music; sweep streets so well that all the host of Heaven and earth will have to pause and say, "Here lived a great street sweeper, who swept his job well."[5]

Questions for Thought

1. How do you think Will Rogers' statement, "What the country needs is dirtier fingernails and cleaner minds," applies to our contemporary society?

2. How can you work hard without becoming a workaholic?

3. Franklin said industry meant to "cut off all unnecessary actions." What are the unnecessary actions in your life that might be keeping you from working hard?

Instructions: This week, devote your energies to the virtue of Industry. Try your hardest to avoid the slightest infraction against it, leaving the other virtues to their ordinary chance only marking every evening the faults of the day.

Industry							
"Lose no time; be always employed in something useful; cut off all unnecessary actions."							
	SUN.	MON.	TUES.	WED.	THURS.	FRI.	SAT.
Temperance							
Silence							
Order							
Resolution							
Frugality							
Industry							
Sincerity							
Justice							
Moderation							
Cleanliness							
Tranquillity							
Chastity							
Humility							

CHAPTER ELEVEN

Sincerity

"Use no hurtful deceit; think innocently and justly, and, if you speak, speak accordingly."[1]

Betsie Ten Boom could not lie. It just wasn't in her nature to say anything but the truth. Never mind that it was the 1930s, her Christian family was hiding Jewish friends in their cellar, and the Nazis were making random searches in the Dutch town where they lived. If the Nazis came to the Ten Boom home and asked her where the Jews were, Betsie told her Papa she would have to tell the truth. Mr. Ten Boom could only smile at his daughter's virtue and pray that she wouldn't be faced with such a dilemma.

But she was. One day, several Nazi soldiers raided their home. They searched the entire house, all three floors of the narrow row home. And when they could not find any Jews, one officer approached Betsie as she stood in the kitchen. "Where are you hiding them?" he screamed into the young woman's face. Her sister, Corrie, reached for Betsie's hand. Their father stood frozen, eyes glued to his daughter, waiting. "I said, where are you hiding them?" The officer yelled again.

"They are under the dining table," Betsie whispered.

Immediately, the soldiers threw off the cloth from the wide wooden table. They shoved the table over, pushed back the chairs, and to their surprise, found no Jews. They were so humiliated that this young woman had just made a fool of them that they stormed out of the house. Good thing they hadn't bothered to look under the kitchen rug; they would have found the trap door leading to five Jews hiding in the Ten Boom cellar.

Those of us who remember being captivated by Corrie Ten Boom's autobiography, *The Hiding Place,* remember Betsie's quandary as if we, too, had been standing in the kitchen that tense day. Few of us have firsthand experience with the pain brought on by the horrors of World War II. But all of us relate to the conflict between telling the truth and telling a lie. We know deep down we should be honest, but we just don't always believe it to be the best option.

> We know deep down we should be honest, but we just don't always believe it to be the best option.

Getting It Straight

In Franklin's eyes, the more sincere a man was, the more he could be trusted and the more integrity he would exhibit in his daily interactions. On the virtue of sincerity, he wrote: "Use no hurtful deceit; think innocently and justly, and, if you speak, speak accordingly." Certainly, this is the stuff of which authentic character is made. In fact, the dictionary defines sincerity as "free from deceit: honest; free from adulteration: pure, genuine, real."[2]

In today's competitive, dog-eat-dog marketplace, Franklin's advice seems tough to follow. It might appear idealistic to think we can "use no hurtful deceit" and still attain success. Too common are the stories: inflated résumés, false rumors, dishonest behavior, or merciless roasting of a co-worker or boss.

It hurts when someone we trust promises to do something, only to later learn that not only have they not been true to their word, they have deceived us. We feel betrayed. Thankfully though, there are just as many, if not more, "honest Abes" making good on their promises as there are con men. Consider the cases of two men.

Truett Cathy is the head of Chick-Fil-A. His personal integrity has literally taken his business from a small corner store to a multi-million-dollar corporation that still operates on virtuous principles. Cathy grew up during the Great Depression. As an eight year old, he sold five-cent bottles of Coca-Cola door to door, then opened a beverage stand in front of his house. His early experiences provided valuable business insight, while instilling the spiritual, social and commercial principles that have since brought him countless civic, industrial and humanitarian awards. Today, Cathy is known throughout the restaurant industry for his ethics and willingness to work long, hard hours: all without sacrificing his family commitments. Of the 500 franchise Chick-Fil-A's, most remain closed on Sundays to honor family and religious times.

Wendy's founder, Dave Thomas, had a difficult childhood, eventually being adopted into a very low-income family. With businessmen and teachers as mentors, Thomas was determined to make his life better. By 1969 he had opened his first, and now-famous, hamburger store. His secret? Always focus on the customer. Wendy's concentrates on its own improvements rather than the actions of the competitors. This fundamental philosophy must be working, because in 1993 the company earned $78 million. Thomas also founded the Dave Thomas Foundation for Adoption and recently wrote the book, _Well Done! The Common Guy's Guide to Everyday Success._[3]

Many men and women have built their empires with honesty, not allowing for any "hurtful deceit." Consequently, their success has come without regret. They live in contrast to their counterparts, whose lives and business practices bring pain and destruction in the wake of success because of how they treat people. Honesty really is the best policy.

Beyond Doubt

Franklin, then, suggests that sincerity not only means to avoid hurtful deceit at all costs, but also to think innocently: give people the benefit of the doubt. If we really want to develop our personal character, we must trust people first until they prove themselves untrustworthy.

A friend of mine recently visited a town 400 miles from her home and, while there, her car broke down. The repair required a part that only one mechanic in town had in his store. She didn't have enough money for the part; but to her surprise and gratitude, the mechanic said he would let her pay what she could, then send the remainder to him when she got home. "Everyone is worth trusting at least once," he told her. She, of course, proved him right when she got home and quickly sent him a check for the difference — and a thank-you card!

Innocent thinking focuses our attention on that which is good and right. Unfortunately, this isn't easy in a society that regularly parades deceptive relationships, illicit sex and gruesome violence. Television is the worst offender. From soap operas to sitcoms, we're bombarded by everything *but* innocence, purity and sincerity. It is especially damaging that television robs our children of their innocence, handing them subject matter that they are not emotionally or psychologically ready to receive.

> If we seek to fill our minds with the qualities of integrity and sincerity, we will quite naturally see those virtues in our lives and character.

Of course, not all television is bad. There are many family and educational shows that promote positive virtues. Therefore, we must guard against what we put into our minds, choosing carefully how we subject our families — and ourselves — to the ways of our own culture. There is truth to the saying: "Garbage in, garbage out."

Thomas Jefferson said: "Honesty is the first chapter of the book of wisdom."[4] If we seek to fill our minds with the qualities of integrity and sincerity, we will quite naturally see those virtues in our lives and character. Through good books, wholesome films, educational television and upright discussions, we can heed Saint Paul's advice, "Finally, brethren, whatever is true, whatever is honorable, whatever is right, whatever is pure, whatever is lovely, whatever is of good repute, if there is any excellence and if anything worthy of praise, let your mind dwell on these things."[5]

Paying the Price

Of course, telling the truth and thinking innocently and justly is not easy. Neither is Franklin's final advice in his three-part definition of sincerity: "If you speak, speak accordingly." Words are powerful weapons with great impact — both positive and negative. Notice Franklin does not say, "when you speak." His emphasis is on the word "if," knowing full well that the sincere and virtuous person weighs his words carefully before he opens his mouth; he understands that the truth one chooses to speak might not always come free of pain.

Recently, employees of a certain company decided to blow the whistle on the illegal activities of their co-workers. Though the public was informed and justice ultimately served, it came at a high price to those who were honest: they lost their jobs and several friendships. In some cases, their lives were even threatened — all for the sake of telling the truth.

However, the great basketball coach John Wooden was right when he said: "There is no pillow as soft as a clear conscience."6 Those who choose to speak accordingly and honestly

> "There is no pillow as soft as a clear conscience."

might pay the price for their decision, but they will be able to live with themselves, knowing they did the right thing. They will be able to experience personal success and respect. They will be living out Shakespeare's immortal words in Hamlet, words which capture the quest for sincerity like no other, "This above all: to thine own self be true, and it must follow, As the night the day, Thou canst not be false to any man."

Franklin rightly included sincerity on his list of virtues for character development. He offers sound advice for anyone in any relationship or situation. Indeed, sincerity presents a real challenge, but it leads to a wonderful legacy. Perhaps that's why our first president, George Washington, once wrote: "I hope I shall always possess firmness and virtue enough to maintain what I consider the most enviable of all titles, the character of an honest man."7

....

Questions for Thought

1. In what way does the dictionary's definition of sincerity differ from your own?

2. What major influences keep you from thinking innocently? What can you do about them?

3. The third part of sincerity is "if you speak, speak accordingly." Franklin did not say "when you speak," but "if," knowing full well that the sincere and virtuous person weighs his words carefully before he opens his mouth. Describe a time when you (or someone you know) weighed your words carefully before speaking. Were the consequences what you thought they would be?

Instructions: This week, devote your energies to the virtue of Sincerity. Try your hardest to avoid the slightest infraction against it, leaving the other virtues to their ordinary chance only marking every evening the faults of the day.

Sincerity							
"Use no hurtful deceit; think innocently and justly, and, if you speak, speak accordingly."							
	SUN.	MON.	TUES.	WED.	THURS.	FRI.	SAT.
Temperance							
Silence							
Order							
Resolution							
Frugality							
Industry							
Sincerity							
Justice							
Moderation							
Cleanliness							
Tranquillity							
Chastity							
Humility							

CHAPTER TWELVE

Justice

"Wrong none by doing injuries, or omitting the benefits that are your duty."[1]

If you listened to my small children — who are nearly perfect, . . . really — you would sometimes hear them say things like: "You give that back, I had it first." "Daddy, he's not sharing with me." "You're cheating, and if you don't stop, I won't play with you any more." "That's not fair."

As I listen to my children — and others, young and old alike — I notice an interesting thing: an innate appeal for justice. It is as if they know intuitively when someone or something is slighting them. It appears that they are appealing to the "Law of Human Nature." The law of Right and Wrong constantly reminds them, and us, to treat others as we want to be treated. It is a law that declares it "illegal" to stack the deck in favor of one person over another. We might call this the law of universal fairness or justice — the cornerstone upon which this nation was founded:

> When in the course of human events, it becomes necessary for one people to dissolve the political bands which

have connected them with another, and to assume among the powers of the earth, the separate and equal station to which the laws of Nature and of nature's God entitle them, a decent respect to the opinion of mankind requires that they should declare the cause which impels them to the separation. "We hold these truths to be self-evident, that all men are created equal, that they are endowed by their Creator with certain unalienable rights, that among these are life, liberty and the pursuit of happiness.[2]"

Though the word "justice" doesn't actually appear in the introduction of the Declaration of Independence, it is obvious that the framers of such an astonishing historic document understood its meaning. They shared a deep personal conviction to doing what was right, both individually and corporately, and so formed a powerful vision of justice for our country.

Of course, this vision has not always been reality. We know too well the incredible injustices that have occurred to Native Americans, African Americans, immigrants and other ethnic groups at the hands of evil men. Throughout our troubled history, we have seen pain and oppression. We've seen "unalienable rights" threatened repeatedly. It seems as if wrongdoing at the expense of others is also an inherent aspect of humankind.

That's precisely why Franklin included justice in his list of attributes for character development. He realized that the fight against injustice was an essential part of becoming a responsible citizen. Because he was committed to doing the right thing, he wrote, "Wrong none by doing injuries, or omitting the benefits that are your duty."

Golden Rules

Justice is a familiar word to contemporary Americans, yet it's a seemingly unfamiliar concept. We all know of the Justices of the Supreme Court, the Justice Department, or the justice gained or lost in major court cases. But when we personalize it, few of us think about "doing justice" everyday. We certainly don't want anyone to wrong us or do us injury; however, we all know how difficult it is to get involved, or to do the right thing when we witness an injustice.

We frequently hear of crimes committed, children neglected or property damaged because onlookers won't get involved. People aren't always sure how they should help or what might happen to them if they do. So they choose the path of least resistance; they look the other way.

But it doesn't have to be this way. Daniel Webster called justice "the great interest of man on earth."[3] For good reason. We will know what to do, when confronted by someone in need, if we simply remain mindful of justice as it's defined in the Golden Rule: "Therefor whatever you want others to do for you, do so for them."[4] In the process, everyone benefits.

Good for All

Franklin wrote: "Wrong none by doing injuries, or omitting the benefits that are your duty." Not only does his advice imply that we must steer clear of wronging or injuring others by our words or actions, it calls us to right the wrongs that might come our way. It is our duty to stand up for justice; when we do, we see the positive results that ensure the inalienable rights of all. We actually wrong others when we forget our responsibility to the Golden Rule.

> We actually wrong others when we forget our responsibility to the Golden Rule.

A perfect example of this comes in an ancient story: In the fourth century, there lived a monk named Telemachus, who was happy and content to go about his religious duties of serving, gardening and praying.

While meditating one day, he was moved to go to Rome, the biggest, busiest, wealthiest city in the world at that time. Telemachus disliked cities but he felt there might be some special act of service for him to do there.

Arriving in Rome during its holiday season, and uncertain of his mission, he let the crowds guide him into the coliseum where the gladiator contests — the practice of pitting man against man or man against beast — were to begin. As he watched the bloody violence on the dirt floor before him — the "entertainment" that ultimately led to death — he realized he could not sit still to watch such savagery and injustice. Neither could he leave and forget what he had seen.

Telemachus jumped up and shouted in protest, but no one heard him as the fighting continued. So the monk raced down to the sandy floor of the arena in an effort to stop the fighting. The crowd thought he was just part of the show and shouted for more violence. Telemachus pleaded with the gladiators to stop, jumping in between the two athletes. The crowd went wild. With their encouragement, one of the gladiators raised his sword and with a flash, struck Telemachus, slicing down across his chest and into his stomach.

The little monk pleaded with his final breath for them to stop as he collapsed to the ground, lying in a pool of blood. He was dead.

Then a strange thing occurred. The stadium grew completely quiet. Shamed silence hovered over the crowd. Someone got up and walked out. Another followed. Soon the arena was empty. Telemachus had sacrificed his life fighting injustice and with an amazing result: It was the last gladiator contest ever held in Rome. Never again did men kill each other for the crowd's entertainment.[5]

Telemachus's commitment to justice came at a terrible price. But it clearly shows us the power of what happens — and how everyone benefits — when we take a stand for what's right.

Friends of Justice

Standing up for justice is not easy. Throughout history, this difficult virtue has often required the isolation, imprisonment, and in some cases the lives of men and women of considerable character and conscience. From Joan of Arc and Abraham Lincoln to Rosa Parks and Martin Luther King, Jr., many important historical figures exemplify the courage and conviction necessary to commit our lives to justice. They prove, thankfully, that a sense of right, good and fairness is worth fighting for. They are examples that can't afford to go unnoticed.

That's why I love one of America's most visible representations of justice: the Statue of Liberty in New York City. What a grand symbol of justice and freedom. There are dozens of letters displayed in its museum reflecting the sentiments of immigrants who, having left troubled homelands behind in anticipation of new opportunities in America, first saw the magnificent statue. Their feelings of awe and gratitude for a new life are worth reading. But of particular note are some of the statements penned by international writers concerning liberty:

"I am content. America is assured of her independence. Mankind has won its cause; liberty is no longer homeless" — Marquis de Lafayette.

"Liberty is not the power to do what one wants, but it is the desire to do what one can" — Jean-Paul Sartre.

"If only I could so live and so serve the world that after me there should never again be birds in cages" — Isak Dinesen.

Dinesen's quote, most of all, depicts an attitude of justice, of treating people fairly, of speaking up for what is right. When this happens, everyone is better off and we no longer see "birds in cages."

In like manner, Franklin's conviction for justice, ought to remind each of us that our country has been successful only because of the rich heritage of men and women trying to do right. Certainly, there is no more important and rewarding virtue for us today.

Questions for Thought

1. In your own words, define justice.

2. In what ways has the Golden Rule shaped your attitudes?

3. How would you interpret the following?
   - "I am content. America is assured of her independence. Mankind has won its cause; liberty is no longer homeless," — Marquis de Lafayette.
   - "Liberty is not the power to do what one wants, but it is the desire to do what one can," — Jean Paul Sartre.
   - "If only I could so live and so serve the world that after me there should never again be birds in cages," — Isak Dinesen.

Instructions: This week, devote your energies to the virtue of Justice. Try your hardest to avoid the slightest infraction against it, leaving the other virtues to their ordinary chance only marking every evening the faults of the day.

Justice							
"Wrong none by doing injuries, or omitting the benefits that are your duty."							
	SUN.	MON.	TUES.	WED.	THURS.	FRI.	SAT.
Temperance							
Silence							
Order							
Resolution							
Frugality							
Industry							
Sincerity							
Justice							
Moderation							
Cleanliness							
Tranquillity							
Chastity							
Humility							

CHAPTER THIRTEEN
Moderation

"Avoid extremes; forbear resenting injuries so much as
you think they deserve."[1]

In the early 1960s, black religious leader and civil rights activist
John Perkins decided to return to his home state of Mississippi.
He couldn't accept the fact that his people were living in poverty,
racism and oppression. He knew he could no longer stay comfortable in his California house while his people back home suffered. He
knew other civil rights groups had organized economic boycotts to
win their "inalienable rights;" so, as Perkins saw the injustices of his
hometown — blacks unable to buy homes or even basic necessities
at a decent price — he went to work by initiating his own boycott.

For weeks, his leadership gained the attention of local white business owners as blacks refused to shop in their stores. It seemed as if
change was around the corner. But then without warning, Perkins
was suddenly put in jail for leading the economic boycott. While
there, he began to understand the depths of the depravity of racism.

White police officers beat him almost to the point of death. Blood
splattered on the floor as they kicked his stomach, "teaching the nig-
ger a lesson." In the midst of such horrors, Perkins asked God for

his life; in exchange, he promised to never reduce himself to such extreme hatred. Instead, he bargained with God, "if He got me out of this place alive, I would begin to preach a gospel that I knew was stronger than my race, my economic interests, my culture, one that could reconcile black and white, Jew and Gentile together."[2]

For the past thirty years, John Perkins has, in fact, worked tirelessly for racial reconciliation — openly forgiving the whites who injured him. He has authored several books and encourages urban organizations throughout the nation to work for reconciliation and community development. Perkins' story is a powerful example of forgiveness and perspective, qualities that comprise what Franklin called the virtue of moderation: "Avoid extremes; forbear resenting injuries so much as you think they deserve."

> Moderation is to the mind and the emotions what temperance is to physical passion.

Keeping Our Balance

Moderation is to the mind and the emotions what temperance is to physical passion. By definition, it means, "to be less severe or less violent."[3] Franklin personally understood the importance of moderation. In his daily interactions he tried to be both cautious and restrained in expressing his opinions. So as not to cause arguments, he would always preface his remarks with, "I believe it to be such-in-such."[4]

To avoid extremes — the first part of Franklin's definition — is to keep our principles and values in perspective. It has been said that error is truth taken too far; one glance at societal problems confirms this. Moderation, then, gives a proper sense of perspective and balance.

As humans, it's our nature to look down on the shortcomings of others. If we don't struggle with a particular bad habit or vice, we are quick to look critically at others who do. For the sake of developing our character, we must fight the natural tendency (like Dr. Perkins did) to be angry or impatient with those who don't seem to care one bit about their character — or the countless problems caused by a lack of it.

Ours is a country often characterized as obsessive, compulsive and resentful. Just think of all the movies made recently about obsessive lovers; all the therapy sessions held for those with compulsive behaviors; and the continuous violent crimes committed against individuals and corporations because of long-held resentments.

Rather than avoiding extremes, it seems America has been bent on obtaining success regardless of the regrets that go with it — on "having it all at any expense." Maybe that's why addictions to drugs, alcohol, pornography and the like have become so prevalent. Sadly, our young people have fallen prey to the same obsessions: In 1990, 1.6 million American teenagers needed treatment for alcoholism and drug abuse.[5]

As pollster Daniel Yankelovich suggests, American society "places less value on sacrifice as a moral good; and less value on correctness and restraint in matters of physical pleasure and sexuality."[6] We all know too well the reality that in today's culture, it is difficult to find balance. The demands for our time and affections tempt many into becoming workaholics, obsessed with physical fitness or engrossed in meaningless pursuits. We need balance to moderate our goals and ambitions. We need boundaries and structures to properly develop our creativity and individuality. We need perspective and balance with regard to our passions.

Learning to Forgive

We also need to "forbear resenting injuries so much as you think they deserve." This second portion of Franklin's definition no doubt had its root in dealing with personal criticism from others. Make no mistake about it, as soon as you determine to have your decisions and actions dictated by principles and absolute values, you will come under unjust attacks, like Dr. Perkins did. Some will accuse you of being self-righteous, pompous or arrogant. Some will consider your commitment to virtue and excellence of character as a judgment against them.

Frankly, we are rather weak creatures. We are easily threatened and too often derive a perverse pleasure from seeing others stumble and fall. So how will we respond when these unjust criticisms come? What should we do when we are injured? Franklin's advice is to forebear it! As difficult as it is, our best reaction is to use moderation. As the great poet George Herbert wrote: "He who cannot forgive others breaks the bridge over which he must pass himself."[7]

One of the greatest examples of this approach was Abraham Lincoln. Few figures in history received more criticism and vilification than our sixteenth president. Because of his physical appearance, Lincoln endured cruel name-calling: "grotesque, baboon, ape, a buffoon."[8] Because of his stand against slavery, he was called things that I will not print here. In short, he endured more than his share of assault on his character.

"Forgiveness is a man's deepest need and highest achievement."

Amazingly, he chose to deal with personal attack by ignoring it. It takes a secure person to respond that way. As Gandhi said: "The weak can never forgive. Forgiveness is the attribute of the strong." However, when someone would make a false accusation that was damaging to the principles he held dear, Lincoln felt he could not back down. He would not compromise; nor would he "be terrified by an excited populace, and be hindered from speaking [his] honest sentiments."[9]

Lincoln had two primary ways of responding. Frequently he would sit down and write a lengthy, detailed and emotional letter. Once he vented his anger and made his defense, he simply proceeded not to mail the letter![10] Having had a good time emoting and making his point, he would just let it drop. In other words, he would "forbear resenting injuries so much as [he thought] they deserve [d]."

In his second favorite method he used humor to defuse the situation. This brought some mean-spirited retribution as well. But Lincoln refused to become like those who were attacking him: spiteful, vengeful and bitter. This policy served him well. Often, because of his unwillingness to take extreme action and because of his commitment to ignore assaults against him, he successfully defeated his enemies — he made them his friends.

Indeed, "Forgiveness is a man's deepest need and highest achievement," wrote Horace Bushnell.[11] To be balanced, to forbear resenting injuries, and to forgive others, these are the qualities of moderation that make successful individuals.

....

Questions for Thought

1. In what ways can balance, boundaries and structure help us in planning our lives?

2. The poet George Herbert wrote: "He who cannot forgive others breaks the bridge over which he must pass himself." How could this apply to you or someone you know?

3. How do you respond when someone falsely accuses you or attacks your character? What might be good advice for these situations?

Instructions: This week, devote your energies to the virtue of Moderation. Try your hardest to avoid the slightest infraction against it, leaving the other virtues to their ordinary chance only marking every evening the faults of the day.

Moderation							
"Avoid extremes; forbear resenting injuries so much as you think they deserve."							
	SUN.	MON.	TUES.	WED.	THURS.	FRI.	SAT.
Temperance							
Silence							
Order							
Resolution							
Frugality							
Industry							
Sincerity							
Justice							
Moderation							
Cleanliness							
Tranquillity							
Chastity							
Humility							

CHAPTER FOURTEEN

Cleanliness

"Tolerate no uncleanness in body, clothes, or habitation."[1]

Not long ago, a clean-up day was planned in the New York City neighborhood where a friend of mine lives. There were bright posters hanging from telephone polls and street signs advertising the activity to encourage families and friends to come out and help clean up the community.

It wasn't like the neighborhood was particularly dirty. Sure, a few empty potato chip bags and soda pop cans peppered the sidewalks. Beat up cars and broken glass sometimes cluttered the streets, but not often. Overall, this was an urban neighborhood full of flower boxes, park benches, green trees, accessible trash cans and leashed dogs. Why the need for a clean-up day?

Because these residents enjoyed their community so much they were committed to keeping it clean. They knew that cleanliness meant more than picking up trash or planting new flowers: it translated into pride, security and an enhanced quality of life. External cleanliness reflected an internal attitude that valued beauty and serenity.

No doubt this was the perspective of Franklin in his personal commitment to the art of virtue. His language was strong when he spoke of the tenth value on his list: "Tolerate no uncleanness in body, clothes, or habitation." Why such emphatic language? Why was Franklin so firm about tolerating NO uncleanness? He understood that cleanliness ensures healthy, confident lives.

Scrubbing the Stains

First, let's look at Franklin's three-part admonition for cleanliness of body, clothes and habitation. I believe Franklin understood early on what most contemporary Americans have been taught since elementary school — personal hygiene prevents disease and infection. The cleaner our bodies, our clothes and our surroundings, the less susceptible we are to the germs and impurities that cause sickness. Someone once said that clean living makes the undertaker wait longer for his money.

Today, we can scrub our flesh with a variety of soaps and cleansers; wash our clothes in bleaches and detergents; and dust, vacuum, sweep and wax our homes and cars. In short, staying clean means staying healthy. But I think Franklin meant more than that.

These three external areas — body, clothes, environment — often mirror what's going on inside of a person. For instance, I can usually tell when my schedule is too busy or out of control by just looking at my desk. Piles of reading material, unopened mail, assorted papers that should be filed are scattered so I can't see the wood of my desk. Whenever this happens, it reminds me that I need to slow down, to get my schedule (and my desk) in order. As a general principle, the external clutter signals an internal disorder.

Numerous self-esteem gurus capitalize on this principle, talking openly about how a person's outward appearance can effect an inner confidence. "When you look good, you feel good," they say. A professional and neat look, they say, communicates your ability to attend to detail. If you have given specific care and attention to your appearance, then you will give that same kind of care and attention to your other responsibilities as well. They provide all sorts of evidence that a neat, clean appearance will "improve your chances" for that new job, that potential date, or that particular promotion.

And they are right, to some degree. Often, what happens on the outside reflects who we are on the inside; however, it's important to keep this in balance. Our society has gone out of control in staring at its own reflection. Who could deny that we are too caught up in beauty contests and mesmerized by glamorous lifestyles, good looks and wealth?

Yes, our appearance matters, but what's on the inside is of much greater importance. We must not let our concern for external cleanliness outweigh our commitment to our internal convictions.

Beyond the Mirror

When we clean up our lives, our chances for true contentment and character development increase dramatically; yet, that's not an easy task. No doubt that is why Franklin's mandate was so clear. When Franklin wrote to "tolerate _no_ uncleanness," he implied a strength and devotion that did not compromise in the area of purity in any way.

> We must not let our concern for external cleanliness outweigh our commitment to our internal convictions.

We have long known that a physically clean environment decreases the spreading of infectious diseases. But in what have been called the "diseases of civilization and lifestyle," we have discovered other ways to pollute our lives. In fact, the Center for Disease Control estimates that more than fifty percent of all deaths are caused by poor lifestyle choices. The rise in stress-related illnesses; pollution-related diseases; alcohol, drug and tobacco abuse; and the lack of sexual restraint all reflect a lack of inner discipline.[2]

"Bad inner-housecleaning," one medical expert called it. Another astutely remarked that "those who predicted the human race would evolve into a communal picture of non-toxic, robust heartiness have been deeply shaken by the statistics of the last few decades."[3] Progress might bring technology, affluence and education, but not the kind of inner discipline necessary for a clean bill of health.

For us all, then, Franklin's advice for tolerating no uncleanness suggests we literally make a clean sweep of the vices and bad habits that hinder a healthy, pure lifestyle. It suggests removing the toxins and contaminants from our bodies and minds in order to best attain our potential and increase our productivity. In all aspects of our life — from what we eat, to what we watch for entertainment, to how we interact with others and even to how we spend our time, energy and money — we must reflect a sense of cleanliness and purity if we are to be people of character.

A person of character knows that it is better to have clean hands and a pure heart than clever hands and a smooth tongue. Steve Hill knows this first hand. Caught up in the drug culture of the 1970s, he developed a reputation as a con man that would cut a drug deal like "butchers cut chickens." His choices eventually landed him in jail, where he was forced to take a long hard look at his life.

> It is better to have clean hands and a pure heart than clever hands and a smooth tongue.

When the director of a local drug and alcohol rehabilitation center offered to get Steve out of jail if he would go through his program, Steve agreed. He was desperate. Judges, police officers and former teachers all warned the director about Steve's "smooth tongue" and that Steve's brain was probably fried from the drugs.

But Steve proved them wrong. After a year of intense personal discipline and community support, Steve graduated from the program. In addition, he became a full-time drug and alcohol rehabilitation counselor, actively encouraging other young people to stay clean. Today, Steve leads an international organization committed to helping people make better lifestyle choices in overcoming their addictions and habits.

Tough Flowers

The results and benefits of clean living are obvious: your physical health improves, your mind is renewed, your contributions to your community are stronger and your potential is unlimited. Franklin's philosophy about cleanliness is sound advice for all of us interested in making a difference in our world. In many ways, cleanliness makes us tougher, stronger and more vibrant: qualities that others will always notice and respect.

Qualities like these were evident to one prominent leader during his visit to a small mining town in the South. While being escorted through one of the dark and dirty passageways of the coal mine, he spied a beautiful white flower growing out of the black earth. He immediately stopped. "How can there be a flower of such purity and beauty in this dirty mine?" the leader asked. "Throw some of the coal dust on it and see," was the reply. To his surprise, as fast as the dirt touched those snowy petals, it slid right off to the ground, leaving the flower just as lovely as before. It was so smooth that the dirt could not cling to the flower.[4]

In the same way, our commitment to the virtue of cleanliness can so strengthen us that virtually any sign of impurity will slide right off of us. The result is stunning, shining and authentically beautiful. Our world could certainly use more people dedicated to clean living.

Questions for Thought

1. What are the rewards of an attitude of purity and cleanliness?

2. A white flower grew in a dirty coal mine. Can you think of other examples of how impurities "slide right off" a thing or person of strength and beauty? What's the secret?

3. Personal Challenge: Conduct a personal assessment of your commitment to cleanliness "in body, clothes, or habitation." What changes of lifestyle will you make?

Instructions: This week, devote your energies to the virtue of Cleanliness. Try your hardest to avoid the slightest infraction against it, leaving the other virtues to their ordinary chance only marking every evening the faults of the day.

Cleanliness							
"Tolerate no uncleanness in body, clothes, or habitation."							
	SUN.	MON.	TUES.	WED.	THURS.	FRI.	SAT.
Temperance							
Silence							
Order							
Resolution							
Frugality							
Industry							
Sincerity							
Justice							
Moderation							
Cleanliness							
Tranquillity							
Chastity							
Humility							

CHAPTER FIFTEEN

Tranquillity

"Be not disturbed at trifles, or at accidents common or unavoidable."[1]

I know what I'm going to do tomorrow and the next day and the next year and the year after that. I'm shaking the dust of this crummy little town off my feet and I'm going to see the world: Italy, Greece, the Parthenon, and the Colosseum. Then I'm coming back here and go to college and see what they know, and then I'm going to build things. I'm gonna build airfields. I'm gonna build skyscrapers a hundred stories high. I'm gonna build bridges a mile long . . . [2]

Unfortunately, George Bailey never did build bridges or skyscrapers. And he never made it to Italy or the Parthenon. In fact, he never made it out of the "crummy little town" known to Christmas-time movie watchers as Bedford Falls. Instead, poor George — in the classic film *It's a Wonderful Life* — got trapped in what he eventually perceived as an absolutely uneventful life; one he thought made little difference; one where he seemed to have little control over his circumstances; and one where little things annoyed him in big ways. Consequently, he saw himself as a failure and came to believe he'd be worth more dead than alive. Of course, he was then given an incredible gift: the opportunity to see what life would have been like without him.

George is a great example of how trifling disturbances or unavoidable circumstances can steal an individual's sense of purpose and contentment. Though George wanted desperately to pursue his own dreams, his desire to serve others and do what was right would not allow it. Still, he grew increasingly restless, anxious and resentful. Finally, it took a lovable but clumsy old angel named Clarence to convince George that he "really had a wonderful life."

Though Ben Franklin never even knew what a movie was, he was all too familiar with a story like George Bailey's. Anxiety, stress and uncontrollable circumstances have been common to human beings throughout the ages, and Franklin certainly had his share. But he was determined not to allow those troubles to stir his otherwise calm waters. That's why Franklin placed "tranquillity" eleventh on his list of virtues, advising us in the following way: "Be not disturbed at trifles, or at accidents common or unavoidable."

Halcyon Days

What a wondrous thing not to be disturbed at trifles, enjoying absolute tranquillity. The image seems foreign, even mythical, to those of us who run from meetings and appointments to family times and dinner commitments. In reality, days of tranquillity (often referred to as "Halcyon Days") seem alien to us. The expression, "Halcyon Days," comes from the mythical halcyon bird that is said to have had the power to calm the waves when it nested on the sea during the winter solstice. On these two days of the year the sun is at its farthest point from the equator and appears to stand still, some say it actually stops.

According to the ancient fable, the halcyon bird had the ability to calm the wind and waves during this time of solstice so she could lay her eggs on a floating nest. Her brooding meant to fishermen that there would be at least fourteen days of undisturbed, quiet waters.

The myth evolved into a symbol for absolute tranquillity where even the sun became peaceful.[3]

When we look at the pace most of us keep in today's culture, the halcyon concept seems as mythical as the bird itself. Quiet, undisturbed days are reserved for vacations, if at all. Life is too fast, tasks are too important, and schedules are too full. Like George Bailey, many of us are caught in circumstances that keep us from seeing how "wonderful" we have it.

The truth is, many of us do get disturbed at trifles as well as at common or unavoidable accidents. We're bothered when we cannot control a situation. We're impatient when things don't go our way. Anxiety builds and desperation sets in. We all know people who are never satisfied, people who complain about everything. Many of us spend thousands of dollars on treatment for stress related health problems. Suicide runs rampant. And then advertisers play on our ingratitude and dissatisfaction, bombarding us with bigger, better, more and now. We long for halcyon days, but we don't know how to get them.

> "There is one art which every man should be a master—the art of reflection."

Learning to Retreat

Samuel Taylor Coleridge said: "There is one art which every man should be a master — the art of reflection."[4] I believe Coleridge points to the first step in experiencing tranquillity. We must schedule time to retreat from the busyness of life in order to reflect on the quality of it. A retreat, for some, is driving to the mountains or walking along the beach; for others it is relaxing in the garden or in the living room. By whatever mode, we must nurture active reflection — halcyon days — to cultivate the tranquillity necessary to sustain, refresh and restore us.

Simply allowing time for reflection often brings about, what a friend of mine calls, "an attitude of gratitude." Being truly thankful for even the littlest of things in our lives — including the inconveniences — creates the emotional equivalent of an endorphin.

Endorphins are those strange substances, produced naturally by the brain, that have pain-killing and tranquilizing affects on the body. The brain usually releases endorphins during times of extreme bodily stress. Some doctors believe that the release of endorphins could explain why trauma victims sometimes cannot feel the pain associated with their injuries.[5]

During times of intense pressure, then, gratitude becomes an endorphin of sorts; so when something doesn't go our way, we aren't nearly as bothered as we would have been before nurturing an "attitude of gratitude." Even the definition of tranquillity supports this concept: "free from agitation of mind or spirit; self-assurance; free from disturbance or turmoil; steady, stable, calm."[6]

Yet, tranquillity assumes self-awareness, reminding us that we don't have to do everything. As we nurture tranquillity, both internally and externally, we begin to understand our own strengths, weaknesses and personality traits. Even in the midst of busyness, we can know tranquillity and rest. Sure, storms and challenges are inevitable, but tranquillity chooses to find peace — to be childlike in the midst of storms.

In addition, tranquillity and gratitude improve our health: laughter really is good medicine. To restore our hearts and bodies, modern physicians are prescribing more and more relaxation and recreation.

Carpe Diem

Let's make the most of our opportunities by seizing each day. We need to fall in love with life; we need to enjoy and appreciate the little things; and we must take time to rest, removing ourselves from the pressures of life's demands. These things bring about contentment, satisfaction and fulfillment, leading us to success without regrets; they remind us that we really can have a wonderful life.

Benjamin Franklin and the other authors of the Constitution shared this vision almost three hundred years ago when they wrote:

We, the people of the United States, in order to form a more perfect union, establish justice, insure domestic tranquillity, provide for the common defense, promote the general welfare, and secure the blessings of liberty to ourselves and our posterity, do ordain and establish this Constitution for the United States of America.

Questions for Thought

1. In *It's a Wonderful Life,* George is given the gift of seeing what life would have been like had he never been born. In what ways did George affect the world? What do you think life would have been like had you never been born?

2. How do you respond to trifling situations or unavoidable accidents?

3. List ten things for which you are thankful. How can this list help you develop an "attitude of gratitude"?

Instructions: This week, devote your energies to the virtue of Tranquillity. Try your hardest to avoid the slightest infraction against it, leaving the other virtues to their ordinary chance only marking every evening the faults of the day.

Tranquillity							
"Be not disturbed at trifles, or at accidents common or unavoidable."							
	SUN.	MON.	TUES.	WED.	THURS.	FRI.	SAT.
Temperance							
Silence							
Order							
Resolution							
Frugality							
Industry							
Sincerity							
Justice							
Moderation							
Cleanliness							
Tranquillity							
Chastity							
Humility							

CHAPTER SIXTEEN

Chastity

"Rarely use venery but for health or offspring, never to
dullness, weakness, or the injury of your own or another's
peace or reputation."[1]

Of all the virtues Franklin espoused, chastity will be the most
unpopular; I am certain of it. Franklin's exhortation is so opposite
today's propaganda that it appears unreasonable. The prevailing
attitude of his day was "either marriage, with complete faithfulness
to your partner, or else total abstinence."[2] In today's culture, that attitude is, at best, tolerated and, at worst, openly mocked. Let's face it,
controlling our sexual desires is so difficult and so contrary to our
natural instincts that either the virtue is wrong or our contemporary
attitude about sex is wrong: I think our present attitude is wrong.

For three decades now, many of our movies, TV shows, novels,
music and advertisements have allied sexual gratification with the
ideas of health, happiness, sophistication, glamour and love. This
association is a deception. The truth is: sex, within the right context,
is very healthy; it can be one of the most gratifying expressions of
love two people can experience, contributing greatly to one's happiness. The deception is: every sexual desire is healthy, normal and

permissible. This simply is not true.

To give ourselves over to every desire leads to considerable negative consequences: disease, unwanted pregnancy, abortion, poverty, concealment, wounded emotions, broken promises, even death; these are the opposites of health, happiness and love. If we really want to be healthy and happy, we need to conscientiously assess what we believe.

We are told incessantly that today's sexual problems are the products of ignorance. We have problems, they say, because we have kept silent; if we would be more "open" and educate people, all would be peace and harmony. If silence, indeed, was the cause of all our problems regarding sex, then ventilation should be the cure: that obviously isn't the case. In our recent history we have done nothing *but* discuss sex; when we look at the facts — not the propaganda — we see immediately that problems still abound. Maybe our grandparents' generation and the generations before them were not so "open" because they knew how volatile and potentially harmful unbridled sex could be.

> It should not surprise any of us that something with so great a potential for creating beauty and enjoyment could also cause pain and heartache.

Natural Desires

"There is nothing wrong with sex," is what we hear people say every day. And they are right, if they mean the natural desire that every human being experiences. But, if they mean there is nothing wrong with our present attitudes and indulgences, I think they are mistaken. Nothing I say should be construed as implying that the sexual act is wrong or "dirty." It is a marvelous gift from God and should be respected and appreciated as such.

We are told that sex is like every other appetite, need and drive. It is compared with our biological need for food, water and air. There is a very important difference though: biological needs are all necessary for sustaining life; and whereas you may believe you will die if you do not have sex, you will not. Indeed, in today's climate, you may die if you do!

It should not surprise any of us that something with so great a potential for creating beauty and enjoyment could also cause pain and heartache. People today are so often used by each other that they leave bits and pieces of themselves with others, confusing love with sex in the process. Unfortunately, over the past twenty years of counseling and working with people, I have witnessed firsthand the debilitating affects that sex, out of its proper context, has on people.

We have failed to define the proper context into which our sexuality should be expressed. We have ignored — to our harm — what thousands of years of wisdom, religion, proven principles and human experience have taught us: unrestrained passions are dangerous. Therefore, Franklin clearly defined the principle of chastity. Every wise person realizes that they must be ruled by a set of principles rather than passions. That is pretty radical thinking for individuals who, these days, don't seem to think at all when it comes to sex.

The Cost of Infidelity

Franklin placed chastity after the virtue of cleanliness, recognizing the need for purity in all aspects of the moral life. "Rarely use venery . . . " he wrote. Venery is derived from the name of the Greek goddess of love and sexual pleasure, Venus; and not surprisingly means: "the practice or pursuit of sexual pleasure, indulgence of sexual desire."[3]

Franklin's choice of words, regarding venery, implies that the sexual act is to be viewed as a purposeful gift — not something to be abused or performed out of selfish desire. It should never bring weakness, dullness or injury to your own or another's peace or reputation. It should never be done at the expense of another person's well being.

Several years ago, a former student of mine, Melody, called me around midnight, hurt and confused. She had yielded to the passion of the moment — to a boy who confessed his undying love and devotion — and given him the one-time gift of her virginity. Instead of the romance promised in novels and movies, Melody experienced the sometimes-harsh reality of a purely physical act. Instead of a sense of joy, nagging shame overcame her. Even though nearly every cultural venue would declare the rightness of her actions, something deep inside her told a different story. Confused and disillusioned, she cried to me, "Everybody made it sound like sex would be such a big deal. Well, it is a big deal all right, a big *bad* deal!"

Melody had bought into the deception that fills our movies, music, television shows, and unfortunately, even many of our school education courses — the deception that sex is no big deal, that everyone is doing it, and that your only concern should be protection against possible physical consequences. We ignore the fact that our sexuality is a very complex and powerful part of who we are; it touches us not only physically but also emotionally, psychologically and spiritually. We mock chastity, purity and virginity as being old-fashioned or prudish, discounting the positive impact they make on the individual and society.

> We ignore the fact that our sexuality is a very complex and powerful part of who we are; it touches us not only physically but also emotionally, psychologically and spiritually.

What Melody experienced was not an indictment against the sexual act itself. Sex should be deeply gratifying for two people in a committed marital relationship. But when that act is performed outside its proper confines, it produces less than desirable results, as Melody discovered. That's why Franklin made chastity one of his virtues. He realized how powerful the sexual drive could be, understanding and respecting its latent potential for harm.

Tragically, modern America has failed to heed Franklin's advice; more than two-thirds of the children born to American teenagers today are born out of wedlock. The rate of illegitimate children born has increased nearly sixty percent in the last decade, with the largest proportional increase born to well-educated, affluent women — suggesting that the social stigma of illegitimacy and premarital sex is disappearing. Consequently, since 1960, the percentage of families headed by a single parent has more than tripled. According to Dr. Richard A. Swenson in his excellent book, *Margin: How to Create the Emotional, Physical, Financial and Time Reserves You Need*,[4] "tens of millions of cases of sexually transmitted diseases annually are followed by cervical abnormalities and cancer, pelvic inflammatory disease, infertility, ectopic pregnancies, teenage pregnancies, abortions and AIDS."

Returning to Purity

Think of the heartache we could save ourselves as a nation if we would adhere to the concept of chastity and fidelity! Patricia Funderburk Ware, Director of Educational Services for Americans for a Sound AIDS/HIV Policy (ASAP), tells people all over the world that "every part of their life — physical, emotional, spiritual, educational, economic — will be touched by their choice to become sexually active. Having multiple sexual partners puts you at high risk for contracting a sexually transmitted disease. And when young people remain sexually active, I tell them a condom will reduce, not eliminate, their risks of pregnancy or contracting a sexually transmitted disease. I don't support distribution of condoms in the schools because it implies permission to be sexually active."5

A leading researcher says it is much easier to get young people to abstain from sex than to get them to use condoms consistently. That's one reason Ware believes abstinence is a realistic option. Young people can control themselves. But they also need to see adults committed to remaining chaste. The dictionary's definition of chastity is: "innocent of unlawful sexual intercourse; purity in conduct and intention; restraint and simplicity in design or expression; personal integrity."6 The word "chastity" comes from the Latin *castus* which means "pure."

David Robinson, 1995's Most Valuable Player in the National Basketball Association, is a great example of personal sexual integrity. In *Sports Illustrated* magazine, he was asked how he remained faithful to his wife in an environment of fame and "easy" women. Robinson responded that if he felt a woman was acting improperly toward him by making sexual advances, he would be very direct and brutally honest. He would make it very clear that he had no interest in her sexual favors. Robinson acknowledged that this might seem harsh and feelings could be hurt, but he determined when he got married that if a woman's feelings were going to be hurt, they were not going to be his wife's.[7]

Robinson exemplifies an attitude of commitment and honor reminiscent of what we know as "the days of chivalry." Chivalric ethics originated chiefly in France and Spain and had their zenith in the twelfth and thirteenth centuries. Their popularity grew rapidly, representing a fusion of Christian and military concepts of morality. They still form the foundation of what many today consider "gentlemanly conduct." How interesting that the chief chivalric virtues were honor, piety, courtesy, chastity and loyalty. The knight's loyalty was to God, to his feudal lord, and to his sworn love; and love, in the chivalrous sense, was largely platonic.[8]

Of course, the ideal of militant knighthood increased with the Crusades; the monastic orders of knights produced soldiers sworn to uphold the "Christian" ideal. The battlefield became a dominant, often bloody, arena in which the virtues of chivalry could be proven. In practice, chivalric conduct was never free from corruption, yet the ideal behind it offered a standard that ensured a healthy lifestyle — one worth fighting for.

> He determined when he got married that if a woman's feelings were going to be hurt, they were not going to be his wife's.

Contemporary Battles

Professional basketball player A.C. Green could also be perceived as a modern day knight fighting for the virtues of chastity and loyalty. At twenty-nine years old, he is earning an income many Americans only dream of. Fame and success are sure tickets for him to have it all — any time he wants it. Yet he has made a remarkable public confession: He is a virgin and intends to remain so until he marries. In fact, Green talks with college athletes, high school students and business executives all over the country about his stand for abstinence, encouraging them to remain celibate as single people.

Green's stand suggests that abstinence just might be making a comeback in these times. The youth organization, "True Love Waits," reports hundreds of thousands of young people from over seventy-six nations making vows of virginity until marriage.[9] And I am pleasantly surprised to see that even the mainstream media, including Newsweek magazine and the *Washington Post,* are extolling the value of what they call "the new chastity movement."[10]

To promote this growing pro-abstinence movement, the Washington, D.C.-based Family Research Council (FRC) launched "Save Sex," an ad campaign featuring successful and attractive young people who are committed to abstinence before marriage.

"It's time for a love that is real and lasting and pure," reads the Save Sex ad appearing in the "College Special" issue of *Rolling Stone.* "That's why we believe in marriage. And why we are saving sex for it."

FRC refers to evidence that abstinence is not only safe but also conducive to a happier marriage. A 1993 poll found that the people most likely to say they are very satisfied with their sex life are married individuals who "strongly" believe sex outside of marriage is wrong.

"This series of advertisements is selling sanity," the *Tampa Tribune* said of the Save Sex campaign. "It is thought-provoking and sophisticated, and it strikes back at the commercial, exploitative rot that the television, music, and movie industries have been perpetrating upon American children."

One of the ads, "Clean Slate," features young people who, though once sexually active, have discovered that "sex without a lifetime commitment is empty." The campaign has also been featured in the *Miami Herald,* the *Washington Times* and on the *Oprah Winfrey* show.

No doubt these current campaigns would have made Ben Franklin proud. They are exactly the type of efforts that promote chastity as he wrote about it; they are helping restore sex to its rightful place and dignity.

Questions for Thought

1. Why do you think safe sex is such a controversial topic these days?

2. Do you agree or disagree with Patricia Funderburk Ware when she says that "every part of their life — physical, emotional, spiritual, educational, economic — will be touched by their choice to become sexually active . . . I don't support distribution of condoms in the schools because it implies permission to be sexually active"?

3. How do you think Franklin's advice to "rarely use venery but for health or offspring, never to dullness, weakness, or the injury of your own or another's peace or reputation" is relevant to men and women today?

Instructions: This week, devote your energies to the virtue of Chastity. Try your hardest to avoid the slightest infraction against it, leaving the other virtues to their ordinary chance only marking every evening the faults of the day.

Chastity							
"Rarely use venery but for health or offspring, never to dullness, weakness, or the injury of your own or another's peace or reputation."							
	SUN.	MON.	TUES.	WED.	THURS.	FRI.	SAT.
Temperance							
Silence							
Order							
Resolution							
Frugality							
Industry							
Sincerity							
Justice							
Moderation							
Cleanliness							
Tranquillity							
Chastity							
Humility							

CHAPTER SEVENTEEN
Humility

"Imitate Jesus and Socrates."[1]

When Franklin was an eager eighteen-year-old, he visited the great Puritan preacher Cotton Mather — whom young Ben had much admired. It was a humbling experience, as Franklin records in his autobiography:

> Mather . . . received me in his library and on my taking leave showed me a shorter way out of the house, through a narrow passage, which was crossed by a beam overhead. We were talking as I withdrew, he accompanying me behind, and I turning partly towards him, when he said hastily, "Stoop, stoop!" I did not understand him till I felt my head hit against the beam. He was a man that never missed any occasion of giving instruction, and upon this he said to me, "You are young and have the world before you; Stoop as you go through it, and you will miss many hard thumps." This advice, thus beat into my head, has frequently been of use to me, and I often think of it when I see pride morti-

fied and misfortunes brought upon people by carrying their heads too high.[2]

Supposedly, Franklin's challenge was much more than merely stooping to miss hard thumps; he struggled his entire life with arrogance and domineering manners. Considering his many gifts, he was often tempted to think more highly of himself than he thought agreeable. In fact, at first, his list of virtues was to contain only twelve until a Quaker friend kindly informed him that he was generally thought of as proud and that his pride showed itself frequently in conversations as "overbearing." So Franklin added "humility" to his list, determined to "cure myself of this vice or folly." Yet, because he knew he could not create it on his own, he went outside of himself and suggested that humility was to "imitate Jesus and Socrates."

Humble Pie

I like to tell my children that a generous piece of humble pie is always good for us, even though it might not taste very good. It's not necessarily fun going down, but it is always healthy and it improves our perspective afterward. The dictionary defines humility as the quality or state of being humble; humble is "modest, meek in spirit or manner; not proud or assertive; expressing a spirit of deference or submission; low in rank or status; unpretentious." It comes from the Latin word *humus,* which means "earth," and *humilis,* which means low, slight.[3]

Notice that humility is not self-depreciating or effacing. It is not insecurity or uncertainty; nor does humility allow itself to be walked upon or manipulated. Actually, most people equate being meek with being weak; that could not be further from the truth.

In its original context, "meek" referred to the state of a stallion that was broken, a horse that had accepted the bit. Far from being weak, the horse retained all of its great strength and power, but this strength was now capable of being directed. Instead of diminishing the horse's strength, "accepting the bit" enhanced it. Now all its latent potential could be realized and not wasted. The strength could be put to good service for the benefit of others.

Likewise, when we are willing to "accept the bit" of proven principles and be "broken" for the service of others, our greatest potential is realized. You see, humility is the result of a realistic perspective of ourselves as we listen to the wisdom of others. Consequently, we learn to "stoop" so we don't thump our heads. This, then, makes us meek, obedient, unpretentious and willing to learn from others. We recognize the difference between meek and weak. Since we don't have to prove ourselves to others, we realize we don't have to be the life of the party: there is genuine confidence and inner strength. We finally begin to feel comfortable in our skin.

Naturally, those who possess the virtue of humility understand its position. Meister Eckhart, in the thirteenth century, perceived the process of humility with regard to both possession and position as:

> Whoever wishes to receive from above must be below in true humility . . . Nothing is given to him who is not truly below, nor does he receive anything at all, not even the smallest thing. If you consider yourself in the least, or anything or anyone, you are not below, and you will not receive anything. But if you are altogether below, you will receive fully and completely.[4]

> When we are willing to "accept the bit" of proven principles and be "broken" for the service of others, our greatest potential is realized.

Learning to Serve

The one who knows humility is in a great position to serve others. I believe this is why Franklin suggested we imitate Jesus. Regardless of a person's religious belief system, the historical man, Jesus Christ, knew what it meant to give of himself to better others. Franklin was not a strict religious man; though he respected his Puritan roots, he was considered by most to be a Deist. Still, he saw the value of Christ's teachings for virtuous, ethical living.

Some of Christ's best-known words relate the call to service — in direct proportion — to humility. Jesus used the parable of the Good Samaritan to teach his disciples about serving. As the parable goes, a man fell prey to robbers and was left to die on the road. A priest came by and upon seeing the helpless man, crossed to the other side of the road, ignoring his plight. What if some member in his congregation saw him associating with *that* kind of person? Then a religious leader walked by. He too ignored the victim. "I can't get involved, they might do the same to me," he probably rationalized. But when a Samaritan man (the social outcast of Jesus' time, the most humble) came by, he had compassion; put the man on his horse; and took him to an inn where he paid for his care. Christ then told his listeners to "go and do likewise."[5]

For the Good Samaritan, humility and service came as a result of deep suffering. He was an outcast, oppressed and despised simply for his culture and class. But suffering has a way of developing in us empathy for others that cannot be bought or taught: it has to be experienced. The Samaritan could identify with the poor man's suffering, and was moved to action. True humility always responds with empathy and compassion.

Jesus also said in the Gospel of Saint Matthew, "Whoever wishes to become great among you must be your servant . . . just as the Son of Man did not come to be served, but to serve."[6] So, to imitate Christ is to seek to serve others. It is opening a door for a friend; helping an elderly neighbor mow her lawn; visiting a sick child at the hospital. There are a thousand wonderful ways to serve others. I particularly like Emily Dickinson's poem, "If I Can Stop One Heart From Breaking." It paints a picture of service bringing hope and help to all involved:

> If I can stop one heart from breaking,
> I shall not live in vain;
> If I can ease one life the aching,
> Or cool one pain,
> Or help one fainting robin
> Unto his nest again,
> I shall not live in vain.[7]

Serving other people is the way to humility. As writer Richard Foster said: "Humility is one of those virtues that is never gained by seeking it. To think we have it is sure evidence that we don't — service is the most conducive to the growth of humility. When we set out on a consciously chosen course of action that accents the good of others and is for the most part a hidden work, a deep change occurs in our spirit."[8]

Asking Questions

The other road that leads to humility is an inquisitive one. That's why Franklin suggested we imitate Socrates as well as Christ.

Socrates said that an oracle of the gods had pronounced him the wisest of all people, because he knew how little he knew. Socrates recognized his own intellectual and moral limits; so, by always asking questions, he sought to uncover the nature of virtue and to find a rule for life.

Interested in neither money nor fame nor power, Socrates — who had been following in his father's footsteps as a sculptor — left his father's vocation to "seek truth." Barefoot, he wandered the streets of Athens in the fifth century B.C., talking with anyone who would listen, asking questions and poking holes in faulty arguments. This style of conversation penned the phrase "Socratic dialogue."

> "Humility is one of those virtues that is never gained by seeking it. To think we have it is sure evidence that we don't."

Like Jesus, Socrates never wrote any books, never held a political office, and never led an army. Instead, by asking question after question after question, Socrates taught students like Plato and countless others. It was primarily through Plato's published dialogues and his disciple, Aristotle, that the influence of Socrates was passed on to succeeding generations of philosophers.

Because of Socrates' self-control, directed curiosity and unwavering endurance, he is considered one of history's greatest moral teachers. He abhorred any shallow notion of truth for its own sake and enjoyed creating confusion by asking simple questions. "Know thyself" became his motto. He suggests that as we know ourselves, we are better able to learn what is really good; we begin to rely on truth and actuality rather than mere external appearances. That's why he spent his time discussing virtue, piety and justice wherever his fellow citizens gathered. He sought wisdom about right conduct so as to influence the moral and intellectual leaders of Athens.

Socrates drew forth knowledge from his students by pursuing a series of questions and examining the implications of their answers. Likewise, contemporary educators understand that the Socratic teaching method helps students develop their own ideas and conclusion by encouraging questions and critical thinking.

Consequently, his teachings, his lifestyle and even his death all communicated a deep sense of humility. He acknowledged that there was always some new insight to be learned, some new virtue to be gained. Socrates, however, was not fully appreciated by his colleagues; his genius for exposing pompous frauds made him many enemies.

When Socrates was old, three of his political foes had endured enough of his challenges, and indicted him on charges of "neglect of the gods" and "corruption of the young." These were false charges, but politically convenient. Socrates was sentenced to die by drinking hemlock. Even his final comments to his judges (recorded in Plato's "Apology") conveyed a humble, inquisitive way: "The hour of departure has arrived, and we go our ways — I to die, and you to live. Which is better God only knows."[9]

Humility requires that we, like Socrates, seek the truth; that we serve others like Christ; and that we confront our own pride and arrogance. Humility is the one personal virtue on Franklin's list that has the greatest impact on others, but challenges us the most individually. As Franklin himself wrote of it:

> In reality there is not one of our natural passions so hard
> to subdue as Pride. Disguise it, struggle with it, beat it
> down, stifle it, mortify it as much as one please, it is still
> alive and will every now and then peep out and show

itself. Even if I could conceive that I had completely overcome it, I should probably be proud of my humility.[10]

....

Questions for Thought

1. How would you describe a humble, meek person? How does
   your description differ from Franklin's?

2. How do you think service and humility relate to each other?

3. How are the deaths of Socrates and Christ alike and different?
   What do they communicate about humility?

Instructions: This week, devote your energies to the virtue of Humility. Try your hardest to avoid the slightest infraction against it, leaving the other virtues to their ordinary chance only marking every evening the faults of the day.

Humility							
"Imitate Jesus and Socrates."							
	SUN.	MON.	TUES.	WED.	THURS.	FRI.	SAT.
Temperance							
Silence							
Order							
Resolution							
Frugality							
Industry							
Sincerity							
Justice							
Moderation							
Cleanliness							
Tranquillity							
Chastity							
Humility							

PART THREE

Living the Revolution

CHAPTER EIGHTEEN

One Nation

Looking in the Right Direction: In, Out and Up

H umility may be the end of Franklin's list of virtues, but it is where we need to begin our character revolution. It requires humility to take an objective look at ourselves in light of the virtues we discussed in Part Two. Humility is needed to:

- admit we are in need of change;
- confront our imperfections;
- confess that maybe we've bought into an insufficient value system or that we're operating on misinformation;
- recognize that we might have wasted years pursuing things that do not, and cannot, satisfy;
- start over and restore ourselves.

Frankly, asking for help is our greatest challenge; it requires an abundance of humility.

If you have read this far, I can only assume that you have more than a passing interest in character development and in joining our revolution. I am grateful for that. I believe each of us has a significant role to play in bringing about positive change for the sake of our country. Your unique contribution is crucial.

We have now come to a crossroads, the place where the "rubber meets the road." All that has been written before is meaningless if we do not take action. What good does it do to talk about a virtuous life if we don't begin to live one? What good does it do to know the defining qualities of personal character if we do not commit to develop them? As the old saying goes: "The man who refuses to read is no better off then the man who can't read."

It is time to move ahead. Now that we have vision for a character revolution, we must develop our individual character by integrating Franklin's thirteen virtues into our daily lives: we must implement the battle plan. This is no small task. Franklin discovered in himself more faults than he originally imagined; but, through the implementation of his plan for self-examination, he enjoyed the satisfaction of seeing them diminish!

The remaining portion of this book deals with practical ways to make these thirteen virtues, from temperance to humility, come alive in us. If we are to live as revolutionaries we must take three critical steps — looking in, looking out and looking up. These three steps will change our lives, as we become men and women of character.

Morality

Before we can go forward, it is important that we are all on the same page — at least in the same book. It is time to state clearly and explicitly what has been inferred throughout this book: *For us to reach our fullest potential and be an answer to the problems that face us as a nation, we must have a common vision!* We must come to an agreement as to what we will stand for and what we will not stand for. Therefore, there must be discussion about morality.

I am afraid that when most people think about morality, they think of something that interferes with, or prevents them from, enjoying life. In reality, living by moral standards prevents friction, strain and stress on the human machine. Morality is the set of rules by which we must live to function most efficiently and effectively.

Morality, in essence, is the instruction manual that provides the best directions for life. Our goal should be to follow those directions to the letter.

If we are smart, we refer to the instruction manual when working on our car because it prevents us from making costly mistakes. It tells us to do one thing when our natural inclination may be to do another. The instructions are there to keep us from doing what we think is best, so that we are free to do what really is best. If we listen to and learn from the maker of the car, we can repair breakdowns and prevent deterioration.

Moral standards, like a car's instruction manual, are designed to keep the human machine from breaking down and going wrong. If we are wise, we will learn from the instruction manual and obey its instructions.

C.S.Lewis wrote:

> There are two ways in which the human machine goes wrong. One is when human individuals drift apart from one another, or else collide with one another and do one another damage, by cheating or bullying. The other is when things go wrong inside the individual — when the different parts of him (his different faculties and desires and so on) either drift apart or interfere with one another."[1]

Lewis went on to explain this philosophy using two analogies: a fleet of ships sailing in formation; and a band playing a tune. He observes that a successful voyage requires two things. The ships will have to avoid colliding with each other; and each individual ship has to be seaworthy and mechanically sound. Obviously, if the ships keep colliding with each other, they will not remain seaworthy. If there are mechanical breakdowns and the steering mechanism is damaged, collisions are unavoidable. Therefore, avoiding collisions and being seaworthy are both needed to complete the journey.

Likewise, Lewis argues two things are needed for the band to get good results. "Each player's individual instrument must be in tune and also each must come in at the right moment so as to combine with all the others."[2] That is the function of morality: to keep people from colliding with each other; to create harmony, and to make sure each individual is in good working order and capable of participating.

Morality directs our steering so as to keep us from colliding with each other, wreaking all sorts of damage. Personal moral codes, as well as social rules and laws, define what we should and should not do. Most people agree, at least in principle, that we should be fair and honest and not steal from one another. The collisions caused by violations of these moral rules are obvious for all to see. Therefore, we need social morality — good laws — and we need those laws to be obeyed. An even greater challenge comes as we discuss the morality of the individual.

> That is the function of morality: to keep people from colliding with each other; to create harmony, and to make sure each individual is in good working order and capable of participating.

At speaking engagements across the country, I have ample opportunity to talk with a variety of people. When conversation turns to possible causes and solutions for personal and national problems, most people point to the loss of personal morality. They realize that fewer and fewer people acknowledge their personal responsibilities and obligations, and that government cannot solve the growing social problems that come as a result of immorality. Laws, though they may be helpful, will not ensure the desired behavior of character. Reduced to the lowest common denominator, it becomes a conscious choice of individual morality within the operative values we've discussed.

In addition to directing our steering, morality is also concerned with making things right on the inside of a person — that the engine is finely tuned and running efficiently. We will never have a just, harmonious society if our selfishness, greed, lust and ill-temper are not conquered. The best laws in the world will not make people good. William Penn wrote: "Let men be good, and the governments cannot be bad; if it be ill, they will cure it . . . Some say, let us have good laws, and no matter for the men that execute them: but let them consider, that though good laws do well, good men do better . . . "[3] We must recognize that only individual selflessness and courage will create a good society. Therefore, we must strive to make things right on the inside and commit ourselves to developing good character.

Look In

I've already stated that humility is the beginning of character development. It takes genuine humility to assess our strengths and weaknesses in order to gain an honest perspective of who we are, who we are not, and who we can become. We must take seriously Socrates' admonition: "The life which is unexamined is not worth living." If we don't look at ourselves, our lives will be nothing more than empty shells and meaningless motions.

Self-examination is a painful process, primarily because of the personal problems it reveals. If we are to solve these problems, we must confront them. Problems elicit a multitude of uncomfortable emotions: fear, anger, shame and guilt to name a few. Confrontation and problem solving produce emotional pain. Consequently, most of us have become masters at avoiding pain! Therefore, to obtain character, we must develop sufficient self-discipline to master our pain avoidance systems. Is it any wonder so few are willing to change?

> We will never have a just, harmonious society if our selfishness, greed, lust and ill-temper are not conquered.

Self-discipline taxes every ounce of our wisdom and courage; while at the same time strengthening them. It is the only true way to growth and maturity. It is through overcoming pain and weakness that we learn. As Franklin said: "Those things that hurt, instruct." Consequently, if we want to be part of the solution our country so desperately needs, we must set an example through our willingness to pay the price for lives full of character.

I believe Franklin was on the right track when he tried to take a daily inventory of the virtues in his life. He was, in essence, examining his daily life. We can certainly do the same. We could begin looking inward, asking ourselves how we fare in the art of virtue. Perhaps the following questions from Franklin's list of thirteen virtues could serve as a checklist when assessing where we are and where we could be:

- Have you exercised temperance this week in regard to eating and drinking?
- Have you chosen to remain silent in conversations, speaking only that which you feel benefits others?
- Does your life feel in order right now, or is it ordering you?
- Have you resolved to keep your word and commitments this week?
- Are you exercising frugal judgment with your money and possessions?
- Are you working hard and industriously in tasks that matter?
- Have you been honest and sincere lately?
- Have you done right, been fair, or served justice this week in your interactions with others?
- Did you exemplify moderation by forgiving someone who wronged you?
- Do your daily habits reflect a commitment to cleanliness and purity?
- Have you taken time out for tranquillity, both internally and externally?
- Have you remained appropriately chaste this week, respecting the good of a special person you might be with?
- How have you maintained an attitude of humility?

Without consistent self-examination — such as these questions require — we cannot grow. When we invest the time for honest introspection, our external circumstances are positively affected and the rewards are great. Think of a time when you spent a few days reflecting on a major upcoming decision. Or a time when you pondered what went wrong (or right) in a relationship. Wasn't the reflective time necessary to provide clarity in the situation? In the same way, those concerned with developing their character must be deliberate about self-examination.

I firmly believe that when we choose to look inward, living deliberately by the virtues we have discussed here, our chances for authentic success increase. When we make positive choices on the basis of character, we decrease our chances for negative consequences, reducing guilt, shame and public humiliation in the process. Character development through careful introspection fosters self-respect, respect for others, and respect for others' property. Life takes on a fresher meaning and a deeper purpose. Transformation of our very nature allows us to enjoy peace of mind and a clear conscience.

Yet we must not stop here. When we only look within, we become so introspective that we're of no use to others. We must allow our "examined lives" to move us beyond ourselves, creating a desire to be "other-centered," thus motivating us to fulfill our responsibility to our fellow man.

Look Out

Let's keep in mind that Franklin's approach to virtuous living was holistic. It integrated all aspects of life: physical, spiritual, emotional, intellectual and even vocational. It was designed to present a complete picture of what we should look like as people of character.

The virtuous life includes self-oriented values such as temperance and moderation, as well as others-oriented values such as sincerity and justice. We must be in control of ourselves, our passions and our appetites, so we can do right by others. That's why we must look outward after we look inward, assessing how our behavior affects other people and how correcting our behavior can free us to help them.

Charles Dickens' famous character Scrooge from _A Christmas Carol_ is a classic example of self-centeredness turned upside down. Scrooge is a stuffy, rich, old businessman, who thinks only of himself and how he can make more money. He needs the help of others to see his error. One night, his conscience speaks to him in the form of a dream, using the Ghosts of Christmas Past, Present and Future to remind him that his responsibility to others is greater than his selfish ambitions.

But on the night before the three ghosts visit the selfish Scrooge, the ghost of his former business partner, Jacob Marley, visits him. His message is strong; a warning for Scrooge to move beyond self-absorption to a lifestyle that daily considers his fellow man. Chains and misery, his eternal lot for ignoring his responsibility of service to others, bind Jacob:

> "No space of regret can make amends for one life's opportunities misused! Yet such was I! Oh, such was I!"
>
> "But you were always a good man of business, Jacob," faltered Scrooge, who now began to apply this to himself.
>
> "Business!" cried the Ghost, wringing its hands again. "Mankind was my business. The common welfare was my business; charity, mercy, forbearance and benevolence were all my business. The dealings of my trade were but a drop of water in the comprehensive ocean of my business!"
>
> It held up its chain at arm's length, as if that were the cause of all its unavailing grief, and flung it heavily upon the ground again.
>
> "At this time of the rolling year," the specter said, "I suffer most. Why did I walk through crowds of fellow beings with my eyes turned down, and never raise them to that blessed Star which led the Wise Men to a poor abode? Were there no poor homes to which its light would have conducted me?"
>
> Scrooge was very much dismayed to hear the specter going on at this rate and began to quake exceedingly.[4]

Marley's visit to Scrooge was only so that Scrooge might escape Marley's miserable fate, a fate caused by a life of selfishness and greed. Scrooge, of course, decides to pay attention to the ghosts and makes one of the most dramatic conversions seen in literature. He is transformed from being self-centered to being other-centered, a perfect example of what it means to move from looking inward to looking outward.

Look Up

Looking outward after looking inward is an essential step in developing our character. Still, it is not enough. There is one more step that puts both in the proper perspective: the ability to look up. Looking up is an attempt to answer why we are here and what is our purpose. Looking up will allow you to understand the direction in which you are heading, as well as the final destination. Your life's voyage will be a failure if you were meant to go to the Caribbean but instead are docked in Siberia.

An honest look inward, outward and upward is quite sobering: it might even be depressing and distressing. The needs in our own lives could be too great for us to handle alone. Often, the needs of those around us seem overwhelming. Perhaps that is why so many people today are re-evaluating the importance of their spiritual life. If America's soul is to be restored, it will require a power greater than ourselves. Faith in a "higher power" allows people to draw from a bottomless well of strength and hope; it assures us that we are not in this alone. We can experience the "rest of faith" and peace that so many attest to. This third look puts things in its proper perspective. "Look in and be depressed; look out and get distressed; look up and be at rest," could be the motto for the day.

Whatever your position on religion, Franklin was convinced that religion, virtue and character were essential for happiness. Rather than disdain the influence of religion in his culture, Franklin felt it a positive constraining force against the darker side of man's nature. "If men are so wicked as we see them now with religion," he asked, "what would they be if without it?"[5]

Franklin, though considered by many in his day to be a skeptic, was consumed with the desire to live a moral life. As one biographer put it: "His was a reasonable science of virtue. His was the morality of social obligation . . . where private morality had its crown in public spirit."[6] He believed happiness was derived from virtue "since without it, man can have no happiness in this world."

But Franklin soon found through much personal failure that his rational science of morality was extremely weak without the benefit of religious convictions. Let me state again the convictions he expressed shortly before his death:

> Here is my creed. I believe in one God, Creator of the Universe. That he governs by his Providence. That he ought to be worshipped. That the most acceptable service we render him is doing good to his other children. That the soul of man is immortal, and will be treated with justice in another life respecting its conduct in this.[7]

> If an authentic character revolution is to occur in this country, we must secure commitment to the absolute values that have governed mankind throughout the ages.

Even Franklin, as disciplined and dedicated as he was, acknowledged his need for a higher power in overcoming his lower nature. He was convinced that the Creator forbade certain actions or behaviors because they were bad for us. He was equally convinced that the Creator commended certain actions and behaviors because they were "beneficial to us, in their own nature, all the circumstances of things considered."[8]

If an authentic character revolution is to occur in this country, we must secure commitment to the absolute values that have governed mankind throughout the ages; the values that inspired Franklin to say that, "truth, sincerity and integrity in dealings between man and man were of utmost importance to the felicity [happiness] of life."[9]

Lewis sums up this discussion on morality best:

> Morality, then, seems to be concerned with three things. Firstly, with fair play and harmony between individuals. Secondly, with what might be called tidying up or harmonizing the things inside each individual.

Thirdly, with the general purpose of human life as a whole: what man was made for: what course the whole fleet ought to be on: what tune the conductor of the band wants it to play.[10]

So we need to look in, look out and look up as we walk this road to virtuous living. This is the foundation from which grow attributes of character. And it is the place where healthy habits can be built.

CHAPTER NINETEEN

Under God

Building Habits of Good

A lexis de Tocqueville, French historian and social philosopher, arrived in America in 1831 to observe the American people and institutions. His observations were written in a two-part work entitled Democracy in America. "It has been described as 'the most comprehensive and penetrating analysis of the relationship between character and society in America that has ever been written.' "[1] In it, de Tocqueville has this to say about the secret of America's greatness:

> I sought for the key to the greatness and genius of America in her harbors . . . in her fertile fields and boundless forest; in her rich mines and vast world commerce; in her public school system and institutions of learning. I sought for it in her democratic Congress and in her matchless Constitution.
>
> Not until I went into the churches of America and heard her pulpits flame with righteousness did I understand the secret of her genius and power.

> America is great because America is good, and if America ever ceases to be good, America will cease to be great.[2]

Alexis de Tocqueville found a nation of people heavily influenced by religious thought — thought that helped produce good citizens. "One Nation, Under God . . . " provided the common values, laws and principles that allowed this nation to grow and prosper. By and large, I believe most Americans desire to be good people. They want to do what is right, live in peace and pursue their dreams. Yet, all of us have been influenced by ever increasing moral relativism — a relativism that has dulled our sense of right and wrong and produced the negative consequences we see around us.

"America is great because America is good, and if America ever ceases to be good, America will cease to be great."

Our salvation will be found in what we believe and how we act. That is exactly why we must develop lifestyles of character by building good habits. A habit is a "pattern of behavior acquired by frequent repetition."[3] If our revolution is to occur, it will be because people like you and me have acquired attributes of virtue through constant practice, or frequent repetition. Every day we must pursue the values of character, such as those on Franklin's list of virtues.

Start Where You Are

To develop good habits, we must start right where we are. Let's be honest. It could be discouraging to take a personal inventory of what virtues are present or missing in our daily lives. We fall short in doing justice; we waver when it comes to humility; we give in at times to temptations rather than exercise temperance or moderation. Yes, we all fail; we all make mistakes. And we continue to struggle. But that must not prevent us from running the race, from becoming disciplined women and men of virtue for the sake of our revolution.

Developing these virtues is like developing any habit or skill. Athletes who want peak performance don't get it by simply thinking about their sport. A runner will run several miles every day or a basketball player will shoot a hundred shots. A corporate executive does not get to the top of his company by dreaming about it; he must work hard every day in the job he has earned as he advances up the ladder. And any artist will tell you they never became skilled at their craft by simply reading about it in books. Though books help, it is the daily regimented work that provides confidence and competence.

Likewise, developing habits of good requires consistent, deliberate attention to character formation. Some may say that it is unattainable — that this life of virtue and character is too difficult. My response to such thinking is, "What is the alternative?" Should we live a "half-baked" life? Should we live a life of low expectations so that we never disappoint others or ourselves? Should we yield to an existence that always settles for second best? That's not for me! And I bet it's not for you! If during an exam you are given an optional question, you may not answer it. But in life that is not an option. We just have to do the very best we can!

It's important to realize that we are all at different stages of personal growth. For example, some of us might already know how to keep our mouth shut, while others still struggle with speaking before they think. For some, living frugally is easier than it is for others. Assess what areas need work, what habits need development, then proceed accordingly. Since we all have strengths as well as weaknesses, we must start our commitment to character development right where we are.

We can start by recognizing what contemporary philosopher Michael Novak has observed: character is "a compatible mix of all those virtues identified by religious traditions, literary stories, the sages, and persons of common sense down through history."4 No one, as Novak points out, has all the virtues; everyone has some weaknesses. Though we are at different places, we can all work on living virtuously according to the universal standards of what is good and right. (For a review of these, see Chapter Three.)

Good Character

Therefore, absolute standards and universal truths are indispensable in our pursuit of virtuous living. We must regularly identify these values of character in order to apply them to our lives. In his excellent book, *Educating for Character,* Thomas Lickona states:

> Character consists of operative values, values in action. We progress in our character as a value becomes a virtue, a reliable inner disposition to respond to situations in a morally good way.
>
> Character so conceived has three interrelated parts: moral knowing, moral feeling and moral behavior. Good character consists of knowing the good, desiring the good, and doing the good — habits of the mind, habits of the heart, and habits of action. All three are necessary for leading a moral life; all three make up moral maturity.[5]

A person of mature character is one who is moral and, with his whole being, can make a clear distinction between right and wrong. He knows, or discerns with his intellect, the right and wrong in a given situation. In his emotions, he wants to follow what he knows to be right and will vigorously oppose what is wrong. He has, through practice and sheer determination, consistently chosen to do what is right, even when he desires to do what is wrong.

Weapons of Our Warfare

There are three "weapons" or tools available to help us become people of character. These weapons are neither complex nor difficult to use. The challenge comes in finding the will to use them. The weapons are: self-control, truth and responsibility.

Self-Control

Self-control is that vigilant watch we keep over ourselves that prohibits us from giving in to temper or wrong behavior. It is the foundation upon which all virtues are built. Self-control keeps our desires and emotions under the control of our will. Its highest expression is demonstrated in submission to an ideal or principle that lies within. It is self-control that enables self-deprivation for a worthy cause or for the good of others.

Self-control's best ally is delayed gratification. Strong character requires two things — strength of will and self-restraint. One of the best ways to strengthen our will is to do immediately the thing we dislike the most. This requires refusal to avoid that which is painful — and commitment to do that which is necessary. Self-restraint refuses to accept immediate gratification when delayed gratification will produce greater good later on.

In his book *The Road Less Traveled,* Scott Peck defines delayed gratification as the "process of scheduling the pain and pleasure of life in such a way as to enhance the pleasure by meeting and experiencing the pain first and getting it over with. It is the only decent way to live."[6]

Delayed gratification can be as uncomplicated as eating your favorite part of the dessert last or as troublesome as overcoming an addiction. It is finishing the task before you go play. It is dealing with your anger before you go to bed, so you can sleep well! It sounds simple but exerting self-control is difficult and painful. Our ability to persevere through difficulties is enhanced greatly by developing an emotional reserve — a reserve based on two strongly held beliefs: "I am valuable" and "I can solve problems."

> Self-restraint refuses to accept immediate gratification when delayed gratification will produce greater good later on.

When we honestly believe in our value as a person, we want to take care of ourselves. We desire to nurture, protect and guard what is precious: ourselves. It is, in essence, self-care. We won't do things to destroy what we truly value, and we will do what is necessary to maintain what we value. A healthy appreciation of our value assists our will greatly, thereby further developing self-control.

Belief that our problems can be solved prepares us for several realities. Hidden within this philosophy is an appreciation that life is full of problems; part of our quest is overcoming them. We come to realize that solving problems helps produce courage and wisdom. Solving problems also provides hope and motivation. Life is a series of problems, which must be overcome; we can find as much purpose and joy in the attempt — to hurdle these obstacles — as in the solution. We discover that, though gratification may be delayed, it is not completely denied! Through self-control we can all experience the emotional satisfaction of life's simple pleasures — in the right way, at the right time, in just the right amount.

Truth

When we dedicate ourselves to finding that truth—and respond to what we find—then and only then will we be able to solve our problems.

Truth is the real state of things: it is reality. It is not what we hope things to be or wish they were, but in fact, the way they are. If we are to restore America's soul, we, its citizens, must be dedicated to finding out the truth about ourselves as well as the "Laws of Human Nature." Furthermore, we must act in accordance to that truth. I want to state again, clearly and definitively, that I am convinced that there is absolute truth and it can be found. When we dedicate ourselves to finding that truth — and respond to what we find — then and only then will we be able to solve our problems.

A clear view of reality enhances our decision making, because our minds are not cluttered with deceptions, distortions and misperceptions. This is crucial as we plot a correct course of action in light of the truth.

We have all heard the saying, "The truth hurts." Truth can make us very uncomfortable. We are inclined to avoid pain at all costs; correspondingly, we avoid the truth if it is painful. To develop our character, though, we must be committed to truth — regardless of the pain. According to Scott Peck:

> We must be totally dedicated to truth. That is to say we must always hold truth, as best we can determine it, to be more important, more vital to our self-interest, than our comfort. Conversely, we must always consider our personal discomfort relatively unimportant and, indeed, even welcome it in the service of the search for truth.[7]

Therefore, character development is " . . . a dedication to reality at all cost."

Even when we know the truth, we must find the moral courage to act in accordance with it! Some years ago, when I was teaching sex education to my tenth grade class, we got into a discussion about choices and consequences. This led to a discussion about the risk involved with engaging in sexual acts outside of the institution of marriage. As you can well imagine, a lively debate ensued. The reality that there are many dangers involved in such behavior became increasingly clear.

The class was nearing the end when one young man raised his hand to be recognized. "Coach," he said, "I believe it's wrong to have sex outside of marriage. I believe, too, that the consequences for people engaging in sexual activity with multiple partners create too great a risk to be a healthy alternative. But, Coach, if I get the chance, I'm going to do it." At least he was honest.

> One of the most difficult truths we face is the realization that most of our battles are of our own making; they are the result of irresponsible choices we have made.

So, it is not enough to know what to do; we must also choose to do the right thing even if it is difficult. And we must recognize that the absolute standards of virtue and character are imparted to us for our own good and the good of others.

Responsibility

My young student's declaration brings us to our third weapon: responsibility. We are so predisposed to immediate gratification that we are willing to ignore reality. This, of course, opens us up to a multiplicity of problems. One of the most difficult truths we face is the realization that most of our battles are of our own making; they are the result of irresponsible choices we have made. To win these battles, we must take responsibility for our problems. We cannot solve a problem that we do not admit we have.

In our attempt to avoid the pain of our problems, we try to shift the responsibility outside ourselves. We have developed rather sophisticated strategies to blame others for our circumstances. Though this shifting of responsibility may ease some of the psychological pain we feel for our irresponsible behavior, it will never solve our problems.

The essence of character disorder is failure to accept proper responsibility for our circumstances. The word "proper" is very important here, because some people accept too much responsibility for their circumstances: so much in fact that they become neurotic. When anything goes wrong, they immediately assume it is their fault. Any healthy person knows this is not true. There are circumstances beyond our control, with which we had nothing to do. Discernment of the "proper" amount of responsibility to accept is one of the greatest challenges we face.

Frankly, all of us exhibit character disorders in some areas of our life. Deep down, at one time or another, we would all like to shift the responsibility for the consequences of our actions onto someone else. To do so would be a tragic act. We would be giving up one of our most precious possessions, our freedom. And isn't that what this discussion of character is all about? It's about freedom to choose; freedom from the negative consequences caused by ignoring reality; freedom to govern ourselves and live in harmony with others; freedom to realize our full potential rather than just exist! If freedom is important to you, refuse to surrender to your desire to avoid responsibility; instead, embrace it as a drowning man clings to a life preserver. These are difficult concepts to hold on to when times get rough, but they provide us with an opportunity to live.

Skill in the use of these "weapons" equips us for the challenges that lie before us. Our character revolution consists of exerting self-control, accepting responsibility, and seeking the truth by which we should all live. If through reasonable and rational argument, we can persuade others to adopt habits of virtue by knowing the good, desiring the good and doing the good[8] — thus ensuring the good of all — we will watch a great transformation take place across the country. People will call it a Character Revolution.

CHAPTER TWENTY
With Liberty and Justice for All

Advancing to Victory

Approximately one hundred and eighteen years after Juan Ponce de Leon set sail to fulfill his vision, one hundred and two people climbed aboard a small vessel named the Mayflower, and set out to sea. For the next sixty-six days, they worked and prayed and talked about their vision: a vision to form a nation where they would be free to work and worship and live as they pleased. But this was not a lawless bunch, interested in self-indulgence and fortune hunting. These Pilgrims were a dedicated and sacrificial assembly, interested in establishing a better life for themselves and their posterity. They wanted to create a society built on justice and personal liberties secured through individuals ruled by the laws of God.

Having no formal rule or authority over them, these free and equal men and women voluntarily entered into a covenant that formed the basis for a new civil government. Their compact incorporated the very principles of equality and government, by the consent of the governed, which became the foundation of American Democracy.[1] Their covenant was based on God's law (The Law of

Nature) and not majority rule, which, in reality, made it a republic instead of a democracy. 2

They built their lives, and therefore their government, on a value system that was not new but old, not fickle but firm, not slippery but sure. It was a value system that had been tried and proven — a system that recognized the equality and intrinsic worth of each individual. Their system, if followed, would produce the greatest opportunity for personal growth and development without denying the same opportunity to others. It was a non-apologetic system of ethics that extended beyond being self-centered to being other-centered — a system that recognized individual rights but balanced them with community responsibility. It fostered individual moral cohesiveness, which fostered social moral cohesiveness.

> They built their lives, and therefore their government, on a value system that was not new but old, not fickle but firm, not slippery but sure.

Their pledge to live by universal principles allowed for the possibility of community: community not as a geographical location but as what Henri Nouwwen calls "obedience practiced together."3 They vowed to obey the principles that were established by the "Governor of the universe."

If we are to restore America's soul, we must revive this sense of community felt by the Pilgrims, renewing our commitment to the universal principles that produce the virtues we have discussed. These are the very principles and absolutes necessary to guarantee "liberty and justice for all." Once renewed, we will establish community as we practice obedience together!

Two Men in a Pew – Which One Are You?

It's time to make a decision. You will decide, by your actions, either to enter the fight or to ignore it. I hope you will thoughtfully consider the reality of the argument that has been made, and join the Revolution.

Though the process might be difficult, and the task seemingly endless, we have much to look forward to. Ours can be the generation that sets the example for generations to come. Together we *will* leave a legacy — a legacy that will make the world either better or worse.

Finally, let me encourage you to continually strive to be the type of person you want others to become. Through personal discipline and dedication, we can help restore character to a great country long overdue for it. It can happen if each of us stays in the arena, remembers the vision, and dares to fight for victory. You see,

> It's not the critic who counts, nor the man who points out how the strong man stumbled, or the doer of deeds could have done them better. The credit belongs to the man who is actually in the arena, whose face is marred by dust and sweat and blood; who strives valiantly; who errs and comes short again and again; who knows the great enthusiasms, the great devotions; who spends himself in a worthy cause; who, at best, knows in the end the triumph of high achievement, and who, at worst, if he fails, at least fails while daring greatly, so that his place shall never be with those timid souls who know neither victory or defeat.
>
> Theodore Roosevelt

Notes

Prologue

[1] Though based on historical facts obtained from the <u>Dictionary of American Biography, Vol. VIII</u> (New York: Charles Scribner's Sons, 1935), this story was created by the author to illustrate a point and is not intended to be historically accurate in all aspects.

Chapter One

[1] James Terry White, <u>Character Lessons In American Biography,</u> (New York: The Character Development League, 1909) 2.

[2] Malcolm Muggeridge, "Jesus Rediscovered," in <u>Conversions</u>. Kerr, Hugh and John M. Mulder, ed. (Grand Rapids: Eerdmans Publishing, 1983) 251.

[3] William J. Bennett, *The Index of Cultural Indicators: Facts and Figures on the State of American Society,* (New York: Touchstone, Simon and Schuster, 1994) 9.

[4] Bennett 10.

[5] Peter Shaw, <u>The Autobiography & Other Writings by Benjamin Franklin</u>, (New York: Bantam Books, 1982) 74.

Chapter Two

[1] <u>Webster's Third New International Dictionary</u>, (Springfield: Merriam-Webster Inc., 1993)

[2] Nancy R. Gibbs, "Murder in Miniature," *Time,* September 19, 1994

3 *U.S. News and World Report,* 25 March, 1996

4 The Webster New Encyclopedic Dictionary, (New York: Black Dog and Leventhal Publishers Inc., 1993)

Chapter Three

1 Commentary by Charles W. Colson. *Journal American* December 30, 1995.

2 Gary Amos, Defending the Declaration, (Brentwood: Wolgemuth & Hyatt Publishers, Inc., 1989) 39.

3 Declaration of Independence

4 Amos 42.

5 Mortimer J. Adler, Aristotle for Everybody, (New York: Bantam Books, 1978) 15.

6 Adler 17.

7 Adler 17.

Chapter Four

1 Benet's Reader's Encyclopedia, Third Ed., (New York: Harper and Row, 1987)

2 Shaw 52.

3 John Bartlett, Bartlett's Familiar Quotations, Sixteenth Ed., (Boston: Little, Brown & Company, 1982) 74.15

4 Shaw 52.

5 Shaw 88.

6 Shaw 84.

7 Catherine Drinker Bowen, *The Most Dangerous Man in America,* (An Atlantic Monthly Press Book, 1974) 16.

8 Shaw 78.

9 Shaw 75.

Chapter Five

1 Shaw 76.

2 Shaw 77.

3 *The Western Tradition,* Programs 9-10 [video recording], Fred Barzyk, The Annenberg/CPB Project, 1989.

4 The Webster New Encyclopedic Dictionary, (New York: Black Dog and Leventhal Publishers Inc., 1993).

Chapter Six

[1] Shaw 76.

[2] All Bible References were taken from <u>New American Standard Bible</u> (New York: A.J. Holman Company, 1973) James 3:2.

[3] George Headrick, "Let's Learn to Listen!" *Kiwanis Magazine,* February 1983: 19.

[4] Headrick 19.

Chapter Seven

[1]Shaw 76.

[2] Shaw 76.

[3] Shaw 82.

[4] Shaw 82.

[5] <u>Webster's New Encyclopedic</u>

[6] John Wanamaker in <u>The Complete Speakers Sourcebook</u>, Eleanor Doan, ed. (Grand Rapids: Zondervan, 1996) 356.

Chapter Eight

[1] Shaw 76.

[2] *Benet's* 289.

[3] *Benet's* 290.

[4] Bennett 59.

[5] Bennett 103.

[6] Carter, Stephen, *Integrity,* (New York: BasicBooks, 1996) 4.

[7] Doan, Eleanor, ed., <u>The Complete Speakers Sourcebook</u>, (Grand Rapids: Zondervan, 1996). 287

[8] Doan 287.

Chapter Nine

[1] Shaw 76.

[2] Shaw 77.

[3] Shaw 77.

[4] Becky Brodin, "Financially Free," *Discipleship Journal,* (July/August 1995).

[5] Brodin

[6] "Urban News and Views," *Urban Family Magazine,* (Summer 1995).

[7] *Oxford Latin Dictionary,* (New York: Oxford University Press, 1990) 739-740.

8 Webster's Third New International Dictionary, (Springfield: Merriam-Webster Inc., 1993) 916.

Chapter Ten

1 Shaw 76.

2 Doan 291.

3 Charles Colson and Jack Eckard, Why America Doesn't Work (Dallas: Word Publishing, 1991) xii

4 Doan 387.

5 James M. Washington, ed. A Testament of Hope: The Essential Writings of Martin Luther King, Jr., (San Francisco: Harper and Row, 1986) 139.

Chapter Eleven

1 Shaw 76

2 Webster New Encyclopedic

3 Jack Hayes, "Chick-Fil-A: Founder," *Nation's Restaurant News,* Feb. 1996.

4 Doan 207.

5 Philippians 4:18 [NASB]

6 Kenneth Blanchard and Norman Vincent Peale, The Power of Ethical Management, (William Morrow and Company, Inc. 1988) 25.

7 Doan 207.

Chapter Twelve

1 Shaw 76.

2 Declaration Of Independence

3 Doan 225.

4 Matthew 7:12. [NASB]

5 Charles Colson, Loving God, (Grand Rapids: Zondervan, 1983) 241.

Chapter Thirteen

1 Shaw 76.

2 John Perkins and Jo Kadlecek, Resurrecting Hope, (Los Angeles: Regal Publishing, 1995) 19.

3 Webster New Encyclopedic

4 Shaw 84-85.

5 Bennett 42.

6 Bennett 9.
7 Doan 105.
8 Donald Lincoln Phillips, <u>On Leadership</u>, (New York: Warner Books, Inc. 1992) 66.
9 Phillips 69.
10 Phillips 81.
11 Doan 105.

Chapter Fourteen

1 Shaw 76.
2 Richard A. Swenson, M.D. <u>Margin: How to Create the Emotional, Physical, Financial, and Time Reserves You Need</u>, (Colorado Springs: NavPress, 1992) 122.
3 Swenson. 124
4 Doan 302.

Chapter Fifteen

1 Shaw 76.
2 *It's a Wonderful Life,* Produced and Directed by Frank Capra RKO Radio Pictures, 1946.
3 *Compton's Living Encyclopedia,* Compton's Learning Company, 1996 (America Online).
4 Doan 307.
5 *Compton's*
6 <u>Webster New Encyclopedic</u>

Chapter Sixteen

1 Shaw 76.
2 C.S. Lewis, <u>Mere Christianity</u>, (New York: Macmillian Publishing Co., Inc., 1943) 89.
3 *Compton's*
4 Swenson 123.
5 Pamela Pearson Wong with Jan L. Senn, "Interview with Patricia Funderburk Ware: Abstinence Advocate" *Today's Christian Woman,* Jan./Feb. 1996, Christianity Online (America Online).
6 <u>Webster New Encyclopedic</u>
7 Leigh Montville, "Trials of David," *Sports Illustrated* magazine, April 29, 1996:. v84, n17, 90.
8 E.D. Hirsch, Jr., Joseph F. Kett and James Trefil, ed., *Dictionary of Cultural Literacy,* Second Ed. (Houghton Mifflin Company, 1993)

(Electronic version from INSO Corporation).

9 John Zipperer, "True Love Waits Now World Wide Effort," *Christianity Today,* 18 July, 1994:

10 "Abstinence – Chic, Like a Virgin," *Christianity Today,* 12 December, 1996.

Chapter Seventeen

1 Shaw 76.

2 Shaw 263.

3 Webster New Encyclopedic

4 Doan

5 Luke 10:33. [NASB]

6 Matthew 20:26b & 28a. [NASB]

7 Emily Dickinson, "If I Can . . . " The Book of Virtues: A Treasury of Great Moral Stories, William Bennett, ed. (New York: Simon and Schuster, 1993)

8 Richard Foster, Celebration of Discipline: The Path to Spiritual Growth, (San Francisco: Harper and Row, 1978) 113.

9 *Compton's*

10 Benjamin Franklin, The Collected Works: Essays, Articles, Bagatelles, and Letters, (New York: The Library of America, 1987)

Chapter Eighteen

1 Lewis 70.

2 Lewis 71.

3 William Penn, Preface of The Frame of Government of Pennsylvania, 1682. Quoted in Sources of Our Liberties, Richard L. Perry, ed., (Chicago: American Bar Foundation, 1978)

4 Charles Dickens, "A Christmas Carol," The Book of Virtues: A Treasury of Great Moral Stories, William Bennett, ed. (New York: Simon and Schuster, 1993)

5 Verner W. Crane, Benjamin Franklin, (New York: Harper Collins Publishers, 1954) 22.

6 Crane 18.

7 Shaw 88.

8 Crane 20.

9 Shaw 52.

10 Shaw 52.

11 Lewis 71.

Chapter Nineteen

[1] William T. Federer, <u>America's God and Country: Encyclopedia of Quotes</u>, (Coppell: Fame Publishing, Inc., 1994) 204.

[2] Federer 205.

[3] <u>Webster New Encyclopedic</u>

[4] Thomas Lickona, <u>Educating for Character</u>, (New York: Bantam Books, 1991) 50.

[5] Lickona 51.

[6] M. Scott Peck, <u>The Road Less Traveled</u>, (New York: Simon & Schuster, Inc. 1978) 19.

[7] Peck 51.

[8] Lickona. 51

Chapter Twenty

[1] Peter Marshall and David Manuel, <u>The Light and the Glory</u>, (Grand Rapids: Fleming H. Revell Co., 1977) 120.

[2] Mark A. Beliles and Stephen K. McDowell, <u>America's Providential History</u>, (Charlottesville: Providence Press, 1989) 23.

[3] Henri Nouwwen, <u>Making All Things New</u>, (New York: Harper Collins, 1981) 87.

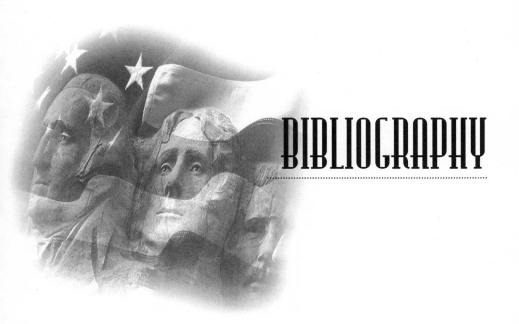

BIBLIOGRAPHY

"Abstinence–Chic, Like a Virgin." *Christianity Today.* December 12, 1996.

Adler, Mortimer J. *Aristotle for Everybody.* New York: Bantam Books, 1978.

Amos, Gary. *Defending the Declaration.* Brentwood: Wolgemuth & Hyatt Publishers, Inc., 1989.

Bartlett, John. *Bartlett's Familiar Quotations,* Sixteenth Ed., (Boston: Little, Brown & Company, 1982.

Barzyk, Fred. *The Western Tradition.* Programs 9-10 (video recording). The Annenberg/CPB Project, 1989.

Beliles, Mark A. and Stephen K. McDowell. *America's Providential History.* Charlottsville: Providence Press, 1989.

Benet's Reader's Encyclopedia, Third Ed. New York: Harper and Row, 1987.

Bennett, William J. *The Index of Cultural Indicators: Facts and Figures on the State of American Society.* New York: Touchstone, Simon and Schuster, 1994.

Bennett, William J., ed. *The Book of Virtues: A Treasury of Great Moral Stories.* New York: Simon and Schuster, 1993.

Bible: New American Standard. New York: A. J. Holman Company, 1973.

Blanchard, Kenneth and Norman Vincent Peale. *The Power of Ethical Management.* New York: William Morrow and Company, Inc., 1988.

Bloom, Allan. *The Closing of the American Mind.* New York: Touchstone, Simon and Schuster, 1987.

Bowen, Catherine Drinker. *The Most Dangerous Man in America.* (An Atlantic Monthly Press Book, 1974

Brodin, Becky. "Financially Free." *Discipleship Journal.* July/August, 1995.

Capra, Frank. *It's a Wonderful Life.* RKO Radio Pictures, 1946.

Carter, Stephen. *Integrity.* New York: BasicBooks, 1996.

Clason, George S. *The Richest Man In Babylon,* Hawthorn Books, New York, NY, 1955

Colson, Charles and Jack Eckard. *Why America Doesn't Work.* Dallas: Word Publishing, 1991.

Crane, Verner W. Crane. *Benjamin Franklin.* New York:Harper Collins Publishers, 1954

Declaration of Independence.

Dickens, Charles. "A Christmas Carol." *The Book of Virtues:A Treasury of Great Moral Stories.* William Bennett, ed. New York: Simon and Schuster, 1993.

Doan, Eleanor, ed. *The Complete Speakers Sourcebook.* Grand Rapids: Zondervan, 1996.

Federer, William T.. *America's God and Country: Encyclopedia of Quotes.* Coppell: Fame Publishing, Inc., 1994.

Fisher, Robert. *Quick to Listen, Slow to Speak.* IL: Tyndale, 1987.

Foster, Richard. *Celebration of Discipline: The Path to Spiritual Growth.* San Francisco: Harper and Row, 1978.

Franklin, Benjamin. *The Collected Works: Essays, Articles, Bagatelles, and Letters.* New York: The Library of America, 1987.

Gibbs, Nancy R. "Muder in Miniature" *Time.* September 19, 1994.

George Headrick. "Let's Learn to Listen!" *Kiwanis Magazine,* February 1983.

Hayes, Jack. "Chick-Fil-A: Founder." *Nation's Restaurant News.* Feb. 1996.

Hirsch Jr., E.D. and Joseph F. Kett and James Trefil, ed. *Dictionary of Cultural Literacy,* Second Ed. [city]: Houghton Mifflin Company, 1993. (Electronic version from INSO Corporation)

Compton's Living Encyclopedia. Compton's Learning Company, 1996 America Online).

Levine, Michael, ed. *Take It From Me: Practical and Inspiring Career Advice From the Celebrated and the Successful.* New York: The Berkley Publishing Group, 1996.

Lewis, C. S. *Mere Christianity.* New York: Macmillian Publishing Co., Inc.,1943

Lickona, Thomas. *Educating for Character.* New York: Bantam Books, 1991.

Marshall, Peter and David Manuel. *The Light and the Glory.* Grand Rapids Fleming H. Revell Co., 1977.

McDermott, Gerald R. *Seeing God: Twelve Reliable Signs of True Spirituality.* Downers Grove: InterVarsity Press, 1995.

Montville, Leigh. "Trials of David." *Sports Illustrated.* April 29, 1996.

Muggeridge, Malcolm. "Jesus Rediscovered" *Conversions.* Kerr, Hugh and John M. Mulder, ed. Grand Rapids: Eerdmans Publishing, 1983.

National/International Religion Report. Roanoke, Virginia, March 18, 1996.

Oxford English Dictionary. Oxford: Clarendon Press, 1989.

Oxford Latin Dictionary. New York: Oxford University Press, 1990

M. Scott Peck. *The Road Less Traveled.* New York: Simon & Schuster, Inc., 1978.

Penn, William. Preface of The Frame of Government of Pennsylvania, 1682. Quoted in *Sources of Our Liberties.* Richard L. Perry, ed. Chicago: American Bar Foundation, 1978

Perkins, John and Jo Kadlecek. *Resurrecting Hope.* Los Angeles: Regal Publishing, 1995.

Phillips, Donald Lincoln. *On Leadership.* New York: Warner Books, Inc. 1992.

Shaw, Peter. *The Autobiography and Other Writings by Benjamin Franklin.* New York: Bantam Books, 1982.

Swenson, Richard A., M.D. *Margin: How to Create the Emotional, Physical, Financial, and Time Reserves You Need.* Colorado Springs: NavPress, 1992.

"Urban News and View." *Urban Family Magazine.* Summer, 1995.

U.S. News and World Report. 25 March, 1996.

Washington, James M., ed. *A Testament of Hope: The Essential Writings of Martin Luther King, Jr.* San Francisco: Harper and Row, 1986.

The Webster New Encyclopedic Dictionary. New York: Black Dog and Leventhal Publishers Inc., 1993.

Webster's Third New International Dictionary. Springfield.: Merriam-Webster Inc., 1993.

Wong, Pamela Pearson and Jan L. Senn. "Interview with Patricia Funderburk Ware: Abstinence Advocate" *Today's Christian Woman.* Jan./Feb., 1996, Christianity Online (America Online).

Zipperer, John. "True Love Waits Now World Wide Effort." *Christianity Today.* July 18, 1994.

Notes

Notes

Notes

Notes

Notes

Notes

Notes

Notes

<u>Notes</u>

Notes

Notes

About LifeMatters

Rolfe Carawan is the founder and President of LifeMatters; a non-profit organization established for the purpose of promoting moral excellence in education, business and religion. LifeMatters' goal is to devise the best means of training individuals in the principles and virtues that promote personal and civic responsibility, and assist them to the formation of right character. Our mission statement reads:

To promote, persuade and train individuals in the manner and means necessary for developing excellent character—for the benefit of the individual as well as the nation.

Rolfe Carawan is fulfilling LifeMatters' mission through addressing approximately one hundred thousand people a year at conferences, seminars, teacher in-services, educational programs and community/ parent programs.

Further, Rolfe's two books—*Profiles In Character* and *The Character Revolution: Restoring America's Soul*—promote the need for and present the benefits of good character.

In addition, LifeMatters offers a successful seminar that clearly defines the purpose and benefits of personal character. Based on this book, *The Character Revolution: Restoring America's Soul,* the seminar expands on the belief that "helping individuals develop character— from the cradle to the grave—is helping all Humanity; a help that is desperately needed today."

If you would like additional information from LifeMatters please contact us at:

LIFEMATTERS
1-800-258-3966